JESUS AND THE RESURRECTION

EXPOSITORY STUDIES ON
ST JOHN XX. XXI.

BY

H. C. G. MOULE,
Principal of Ridley Hall, Cambridge

Third Edition

Wipf & Stock
PUBLISHERS
Eugene, Oregon

Wipf and Stock Publishers
199 W 8th Ave, Suite 3
Eugene, OR 97401

Jesus and the Resurrection
Expository Studies on St. John 20 & 21
By Moule, Handley C.G.
ISBN 13: 978-1-55635-255-3
ISBN 10: 1-55635-255-7
Publication date 2/5/2007
Previously published by Seeley & Co., 1898

CONTENTS.

		PAGE
I.	THE DISCIPLES	1
II.	MARY MAGDALENE	11
III.	PETER AND JOHN	24
IV.	MARY AND THE LORD	43
V.	FROM THE GARDEN TO THE CHAMBER	63
VI.	THE LORD IN THE CHAMBER	83
VII.	THE EASTER MESSAGE—THOMAS	105
VIII.	THOMAS AND THE LORD	121
IX.	THE NIGHT ON THE LAKE	139
X.	JOY IN THE MORNING	152
XI.	THE MORNING MEAL—LOVEST THOU ME?	167
XII.	THE MASTER AND HIS SERVANTS	185
	APPENDICES	207

JESUS
AND
THE RESURRECTION

I

THE DISCIPLES.

MANY years ago—it was in 1869—I received a kind letter from the late Lord Chancellor Hatherley, formerly Sir W. Page Wood. I had been much helped in thought and faith by his small but valuable book, as well worthy of attentive study now as ever, *The Continuity of Scripture*,[1] and I ventured to thank him. His reply contained the following sentences:

"I thought that many young and ardent minds become embroiled in controversy before they have had the thought or inclination to make *proof* of Scripture by its effects on their own hearts when read with a simple, prayerful wish to believe. In my youth (I cannot express the benefit thus derived from Holy Writ) I used, when under trial, to read say two or three

[1] Murray, 1868.

chapters of the New Testament, specially the closing chapters of the Gospel of St John, and never found my doubts so cleared as by that expedient. I have now for more than thirty years perused the whole Volume yearly. I fear I may not have time now allowed me to expose the very shallow reasoning powers of some very eminent continental scholars. Their learning I admire; but at the bar we often find a man's logic swamped by his learning; and so it is in divinity."

I quote these words of that good man and great judge, one of the greatest of all our masters of legal evidence, to introduce a few short studies on these same last pages of St John. Their object is not criticism specially, nor speculation, but reverent verbal enquiry, carried on " with the simple, prayerful wish to " realize, and so the more gladly to " believe." Whatever such studies do, or fail to do, may they lead us a little nearer to Him who is the Life and the Light—Jesus Christ, our Sacrifice, our Hiding-place, our Resting-place; our Strength for watching and for work; our Panacea for all temptation; our Resurrection; our Heaven in prospect.

We begin with a translation:

Now on the first day of the week Mary of Magdala comes early, while it was still dusk, to the tomb, and sees the stone taken out of the tomb. So she runs and comes to Simon Peter, and to the other disciple, whom Jesus loved, and says to them, They have taken the Lord out of the tomb, and we do not know where they have put Him. So they went out, Peter and the other disciple, and set out for (ἤρχοντο εἰς) the tomb. So they were running (ἔτρεχον), the two together; and now the other disciple ran forward (προέδραμε), quicker than Peter, and came first to the tomb; and, stooping from the side, he sees lying the linen cloths. He did not go in, however. So Simon Peter comes, following him, and went into the tomb, and views (θεωρεῖ) the linen cloths lying, and the napkin that was over His head, not lying with the linen cloths, but apart, rolled up and put in a separate place. So the other disciple, who came first to the tomb, then went in, and he saw, and believed. For not as yet did they know the Scripture, that of necessity He would rise from the dead.

Verse 1. Τῇ δὲ μιᾷ (*Now on the first day*). We observe the connecting "*now*," δὲ. It points to previous details, and reminds us that the Resurrection is indissolubly linked, in significance as in fact, to what precedes—the Cross. It is these two which make the one glory of the work of Christ. It is "the Living One *who became dead*" (Rev. i. 18) who is our Peace, and can lay His hand on us and say, "Fear not."

So this brief particle leads us back, over some forty hours, to that mid-afternoon of the Friday when the Lord expired; to the short interval before sunset, when Joseph and Nicodemus had buried Him in the adjoining garden, watched, perhaps from under the city wall,[1] by some of the Galilean women; then to the hushed interval of that sunset, and evening, and night, and following day. That interval the disciples spent in grief and tears, and apparently in different places, isolated into groups. For Peter and John, having with them no doubt the Lord's Mother, seem to have been found apart from the rest when Mary Magdalene sought them; and Thomas was definitely withdrawn; and the women, again, appear to have set out, on the Sunday morning, from different points. Then

[1] I venture to assume the rightness of "General Gordon's site" of the Crucifixion, outside the Damascus Gate. An interesting controversy has lately (1892) been carried on in *The Times* and other papers, over the question whether an old tomb near that site is or is not the very tomb of Joseph. The weighty judgment of Canon Tristram is given for a probable affirmative.

we are led to the evening of our Saturday—the close of their Sabbath—when, as the sun set, the women, or some of them, at once set out to buy and to prepare the odours with which to complete the work of Nicodemus. So we reach the middle of that night, and the breaking of the First Day morning, when from their various lodging-places the women came—Mary of Magdala, Mary "of Joseph," Salome, and perhaps others too.

As we review that interval, I would touch on one point only in the picture of the disciples drawn for us in the Gospel narrative; I mean the collocation and the contrast, so startling yet so deeply truth-like, of the total failure of their faith and the survival of their love.

When the Lord rose, perhaps no living person, excepting (surely) His Mother,[1] consciously and intelligently "believed on His Name." No living person, except her, trusted His promise to rise again, and understood His death in the light of it, resting the soul upon His sacrifice. So this very passage tells us, in regard of no less personages than John and Peter. But such a statement would have been the very last

[1] And possibly the Family of Bethany. None of them appear at the tomb. I owe this remark to the suggestion of the Rev. G. F. W. Munby.

thing which a fabricator would have excogitated, and the very last which would have arisen unconsciously in minds (such as many historical critics assume all the minds of the primeval Church to have been) pregnant with legend, or facile vehicles for the growth of myths. Who in that simple age, with its literary "helplessness," would have thought of *constructing* an utter collapse of faith in the central circle of the disciples just when Jesus was accomplishing His alleged victory—a collapse just *because of* the Cross, which so soon became somehow the hope and glory of His followers?

But knowledge and reflection now show us how true to history, to time, and conditions, and the human soul, all this picture is. All the prepossessions of those men and women, and their cherished wishes, lay in the direction of a triumph not through death at all. The attention they ought to have given to their Master's words about His death had been all the while distracted and neutralized by these intense expectations and preferences. When the stern fact of the Crucifixion came, their confidence was not only surprised, but crushed; and so it would have remained, if Jesus had not risen again.

And yet—they loved Him. They must have been tortured with worse than doubts about His

Messianic character, if, indeed, in those distressing hours they had mental leisure to *doubt* amidst their absorbing *grief.* But *some* formidable questionings, not only about Him, but about all they had known or hoped about God, must have mingled with their tears. And yet—they loved Him. Women, Apostles, all, in one degree or another, they loved Him still. And in this too there is a deep and verifiable truth of the human heart. Mere grief and alarm may easily be imagined over the unlooked-for death of any strong leader. But the leader these persons had lost was JESUS—the Man JESUS, such as the Gospels draw Him. Such a Chief, even had He misled them in the end, must still (it is true in the logic of the heart, which alone is in question here) be loved, for the time, with an intensity only the greater for His fall. Take the case of Magdalene. Jesus, contrary to her dearest longings and most confident expectations, had died:—what could she believe? But Jesus, whatever else had happened, had liberated her from awful physical and mental suffering (Mark xvi. 9):—how could she not love?

May I draw a somewhat evident lesson? Let us give continual thanks for the broad, strong foundations of fact and reason, of cogent and manifold proof, which lie beneath the assertion of the Creed, that He who died for our sins rose again the third day. History has nothing else in it so firm and solid, in the historical sense, as that position. But the human mind is a strange and subtle thing, and it is possible that we may, in certain states of it, find ourselves doubting, as it were, against our reason; seeing the steps and links, but so as to fail to combine them at the moment into a result of conscious and invigorating certainty. Then let us be thankful indeed if we bear about in us another part of the vast evidence of Christianity, that is, of Jesus Christ; the thing which kept the adherence of those disciples tenacious when for a dark season their full faith was gone. This Jesus Christ has, somehow, touched, and changed, and set free my soul, my being. He, and only He—His Name, His Person—has had a power over me which is like nothing else. The more I have seen, trusted, loved Him, the more always I have stood clear of sin, of self. I cannot but love Him still. And as for these haunting doubts, I will at least drag them into the light of His love, and look at them there. If I feel for a sad moment, "They have taken away my Lord," I will at that very moment remember why, among other reasons, I can call Him "my Lord" at all; He, or if not He, then nothing, has freed me from many more than seven sins. Is not doubt about such a Power a self-detected fallacy already?

But on the other side, we must not press too far the resemblance between Mary's case and our own. What was, after all, this passionate love of the disciples when their faith was gone? In a great measure, it was only passionate. It was affection for a Being whom they had (on their then hypothesis, Luke xxiv. 21) much mistaken; affection for some one who, if the faith had been "vain," was less than the Son of God; affection indeed for Jesus of Nazareth, but for a Jesus infinitely short of His reality—a dead, a vanished, a disappointed Friend.

So, warm as it was, that love could not well have persisted. As time went on it must have been infected with the bitterness of an ever-growing pain at the loss, the blank, *the mistake*. Many of the company would be tempted to forget Him, if they could. Some would have come to dread, perhaps even to hate, the spectre of His memory. Those who still loved would love on, not in joy and strength, but in gloom. It was the love more of nature than of grace— let us not fear to say it—which brought Mary to the tomb. The heavenly love—the joyful, holy, undecaying love—was yet to come: love stirred from its depths by light and power divine. But in order to this she had yet to know Jesus as the Risen One, who was dead, but is alive for evermore.

As such we know Him, and have felt His power.

Let us stand by the side of Mary of Magdala, with that knowledge and consciousness in our grateful hearts. Let us look into that tomb, and see it full of light—the seat of Angels, the gate of heaven. Let us turn round with her, and see the reason of it all—the Lord Jesus risen indeed; Jesus calling us by our name, while we answer, *Rabboni*, My Master, O my Master!

II

MARY MAGDALENE.

IN the previous chapter mention was made of the "three days" which came between the Lord's death and His resurrection, the silent interval referred to in the δὲ of our ver. 1. Let us so far return to that point as to remind ourselves of the extreme importance to us of that interval from one particular point of view. "The third day I will rise again"; that promise of delay was pregnant with many mercies. Putting aside all thought and question (never by us on earth to be answered with certainty) what the Lord Jesus Himself might have to do in that mysterious time, we see at once that the interval was momentous, not only for our greater assurance of His literal death, but—this is the point here in my mind—for our better appreciation of the real state of mind of His followers. Their blank surprise, their despair, their mistakes, their broken faith but not broken love—

all are before us now, for all had time to come out. And thus we are able to estimate better the massive solidity of the evidence of the Resurrection, looking at the absolute contrast between the former and after states of the disciples. The disciples between the Friday and the Sunday—the disciples after the Sunday, thenceforward for ever—what a difference! Before, all is misunderstanding, bewilderment, helplessness; after, all is one strong consistency (if we except a passing check, soon much more than repaired, in the case of one person, Thomas) of holy certainty, peace, energy, and joy.

But now we draw near the scene of Resurrection.

Perhaps it was soon after midnight, the vernal midnight, that the Lord arose. Indeed, as soon as the sun of Saturday had set, and the first moments of the First Day had come, the letter of His promise permitted Him to return; for the νυχθήμερον (the twenty-four hours) could be represented by ever so small a fraction of its course. But as a fact the Revival took place not long before the discovery of its occurrence. In one place (Mark xvi. 9) we read distinctly that "Jesus rose early" (πρωΐ), in the early morning, on the first day of the week. It was probably a very silent Resurrection. It was not till the great Angel, afterwards, came down that the stone was rolled fairly away, and the earth shaken around the place of burial. It may be that in a way unknown to us, and unknowable, the Body of the Resurrection was made able to pass through the stone while the stone yet lay unmoved in the doorway.[1] But, however, It passed out from the cell. HE stood up, in His veritable, immortal Body, dropping aside, so that they lay on the floor, just as and where they had been worn, the long linen cloths which had so recently pressed "an hundred pound weight" of spices round His lacerated limbs[2]; and so He re-appeared, "in the power of an indissoluble life," "according to the working whereby He is able even to subdue all things unto Himself" (Heb. vii. 16 ; Phil. iii. 21).

[1] I own the greatness of the difficulties which beset this theory, which *seems* to put an essential difference between the Lord's Risen Body and our body. Yet it must be observed that the theory does not suppose the contradiction of any apparent necessary law of thought. It does not suppose any ubiquity, or practical ubiquity, of the Body, nor that the same space would be occupied by the atoms of the stone and of the Body ; but that the sacred material of the Body was so subtilized by the action of the Lord's Spirit that the dense stone became, relatively to It, a network of large interstices. See further below, p. 87.

[2] Where had the spices gone? Had they been, as it were, consumed by that contact?

In that resurrection life "He dieth no more." The human Form, flesh and bones, which stepped forth in the light of dawn into Joseph's garden that wonderful morning, was alive eternally. Identical in continuity with the Body of His birth and His death, it was in a state infinitely new, "a spiritual Body." For it, time was as it were no more. Eighteen centuries have not worn it into age, nor shall the coming æons do so. In it, He is "this same Jesus," yesterday, to-day, and when He comes again. And every moment of its holy permanence is proof both that we are accepted in His death and are being saved for ever "in His life" (Rom. v. 10).

So did the Risen Saviour triumph in the deep silence of that early morning. Meanwhile the disciples were weeping and groaning because of His death, and were coming to bid His remains the last farewell.

Verse 1. *On the first day of the week*, τῇ μιᾷ τῶν σαββάτων. The Greek plural σαββαθά is a transliteration of the Aramaic *shabbâthâ*, and has no plural meaning. Μιᾷ for πρώτῃ is Hebraistic.

Cometh Mary the Magdalene, Mary of Magdala, or Migdol, a place (probably) near Tiberias, and still perhaps to be identified. This much-favoured disciple is mentioned fourteen times in the Gospels, and always (except only Luke viii. 2, where she is seen, along with "many other women," accompanying the Lord through Galilee, and assisting Him with her personal means) in connexion with the story of the Passion. There is no real evidence to identify her with the "woman that was a sinner." From the Magdalene (Mark xvi. 9) Jesus had "cast out seven devils." But this tells us nothing for certain of any special impurity in her life. All it does is to account most instructively and nobly for her deep, devoted, energetic love. That love began with this simple but mighty motive—gratitude for immense blessings, profoundly certain to her consciousness. She had been a tortured, perhaps a terrible, demoniac; now she was at rest, and Jesus was the cause. So she came to the sepulchre early, in the dusk, earlier than the Apostles; brought by no superhuman courage, but by grateful love.

She did not come alone. "The other Mary," wife of Clopas, mother of James the Less and very possibly sister of the Virgin,[1] was with her; and other women came to the same spot about the same hour, Johanna and Salome among them. But, with one minute exception, which

[1] See Smith's *Dictionary of the Bible*, s. v. "Mary of Clopas."

we shall notice as it comes, their presence does not appear in this narrative. In it we have the whole scene from *Mary's* point of view; and deeply truth-like it is, when we remember Mary's condition of feeling, that that point of view should have regarded herself and her own experiences alone. As she told the sacred incidents over, when she went to the disciples with the message that "she had seen the Lord," she would speak as one whose whole being had been concentrated on what He had said to *her*.

She came *early, while it was still dusk, to the sepulchre;* finding her way to the walled garden whither she had seen Joseph and Nicodemus convey the Body, and there deposit it, rolled in that mass of linen-folded spicery, inside the chamber cut in the rock, at the back or the side of the enclosure. The sun was near his rising; but it was dusk still in the nooks and corners of the place.

And now, *she sees the stone taken out of the sepulchre.* This view, very probably, was not from the garden itself. A glance as she approached it would be enough to show her the black void recess. And perhaps, accordingly, she did not now go up to the tomb at all, but hastened on alone, leaving whoever might have come with her, or have met her, to follow or not as it might happen.

However, the stone was moved. "*The* stone," says St John, though he had said nothing about a stone before. To be sure, the definite article may be accounted for by the fact that every rock tomb would have *its* stone. But knowing as we do from the other Gospel narratives how large a part "the stone" did play on that momentous morning, I cannot help seeing here one of the many details in which St John, in his Gospel, *takes for granted* the main Evangelic narrative, and passingly and without anxiety uses his reader's knowledge of it.

Verse 2. *So Mary runs.* How much eager speed there was that hour! The holy woman, the two Apostles, all *run*, from the sepulchre, or to it, in the self-oblivion of great grief or of great hope.

And she comes to Simon Peter, and to the other disciple whom Jesus loved; so John describes himself, with a *naïveté* inimitable, and altogether unlike a fabricator (when we have regard to the literary conditions of the early generations of Christianity[1]), about fourteen times.

[1] It cannot be too often remembered, when we study the inner marks of the authenticity of the Scripture narra-

So she found Peter and John in company; perhaps in the same house, though the repetition of the πρὸς before τὸν ἄλλον μαθητήν *slightly* suggests that she may have called at two doors. Very beautiful is the sight of this special intimacy of the two Apostles. We seem to see it first when they go (Luke xxii. 8) to prepare the room for the Last Passover; then, when they stand together at the door of the Palace of the Priest; again in this incident; again in the following chapter, and again and again in the early passages of the Acts. How different was each from each—how helpful each to each manifestly became! And we may specially note how deeply "the disciple whom Jesus loved" had learnt in that wonderful friendship to "love his brother also." John had never actually denied his Lord; Peter, probably in John's hearing, had repeatedly denied Him. Many a "saint" of later days would, I fear, have thrust Peter away from all fellowship with himself. But not so John. At once, before the Resurrection, before the hope of it, while there was yet no joy in his own heart, John has joined himself to Peter; has

---

tives, of both Testaments, that anything like finished and really deceptive personation of the past (if I may use the phrase) is a very modern literary phenomenon. Is it much older than Sir Walter Scott?

taken him to be his brother as well as the Virgin to be his mother.

If for us, in our day, the sense of our Redeemer's love, our rest upon the bosom of His forgiving friendship, does anything, it will make us condemn and renounce the spiritual self-righteousness which shuts up sympathy. It will make us feel how wonderfully welcome to the Lord is "whosoever cometh," even if he comes fresh from some grievous fall, some denial of the blessed Name. It will make us so far like Him who loved us, that while we shall see and feel sin, as sin, more and more keenly and painfully (and not least, the sin of not loving the Lord Christ, and submitting the whole being to Him), we shall more and yet more truly love, and seek to help, others for whom our aid may avail, however strange the case, however great the fall.

So, to Peter and to John, Mary of Magdala comes running.

And she says to them, They have taken the Lord out of the sepulchre, and we do not know where they have put Him.

I turn the aorists by perfects; not of course forgetting an important grammatical difference; but remembering that the genius of the Greek tongue places an act or event in the complete past more promptly than the genius of English. Accordingly we have often, for the sake of English, to represent the Greek completed past by the English past connected with the present.

They have taken. The expression is quite indefinite. It appears to be fairly equivalent to the *on* of French ; *on a enlevé le Seigneur;* Joseph, Joseph's servants, any one, had done it. Mary may have thought of the soldiers, who had already left the place pell-mell. But probably she did not even know of their having been there, nor of the seal upon the stone. The guard had not been sent to the place till the Sabbath ; and the women had kept the Sabbath most strictly (Luke xxiii. 5, 6[1]), moving about very little.

They have taken away THE LORD ; wonderful word ! It was only the Corpse ; yes, but to Mary this was JESUS. And she was right. The body, as much as the soul, is an integral part of perfect man : it is so with the Christian, it was so with Christ. We are amply justified in mourning, loving, honouring the precious bodies of our departed dear ones ; they *are* a part of *them*. And truly we are justified in longing, in praying, for the Resurrection hour

[1] Their Master, it appears, had taught them no neglect of the Commandments.

when they shall actually, and eternally, be part of them again.

And WE *do not know where they have put Him.* Here, surely, we have a distinct, though minute, indication of the presence of other seekers along with Mary. Some even devout scholars (I think Dr Sanday is among them) say that we cannot argue thus; that the memory of the aged Apostle could not charge itself with the presence or absence of a mere syllable (a mere μεν, if Mary spoke Greek). But it seems obvious to remark that to recall a syllable may mean much more than merely to recall the sound. The word is bound up with the thing. Not so much the sounds spelt οἴδαμεν cling to the mind as the represented idea of the more-than-one who "did not know."

Anywise, St John has carefully written οἴδαμεν, "we know," and (to speak of no deeper considerations) it is in harmony with his whole style to imply details which he leaves unrecorded, because recorded otherwise already. I take it that he makes Mary here conscious of having approached the sepulchre with her friend, and now to refer to their united thought.

We know not where they have put Him. What strange words, at such a moment! What a sublime "irony," in the Greek sense of that word, about them! Let us try to enter into the anguish and bewilderment of this blessed forerunner of our faith and lover of our Lord. Intensely devoted to the Person of Jesus; bound to Him by ties of the tenderest gratitude, by her knowledge that reason, and rest, and friends, were all the special gift of Him who had disencumbered her soul of the seven foul spirits; bound to Him also by longing hopes, cherished visions (in the light of true prophecy) of His passionless triumph and worldwide glory and fame; longing, no doubt, for all this wholly for His sake, and not at all for her own; she now saw Him murdered, buried, and—stolen from her. And her only resource was to run to two poor men, as hopeless and helpless as herself, and even more paralysed. And yet, she loves. She is energized by love; she will still do anything for "the Lord."

How shall it be with us? We know immeasurably more (it is strictly true) about Christ Jesus than Mary at that moment did. We know him as the Eternal SON given for our sins, according to the Scriptures. We know Him as the Risen One, according to the Scriptures, living at this hour—and for ever—for us, with us, in us. He is revealed to us as the Ascended One, our Mediator and Head at the right hand of Eternal Love. Ah, what should be our thanksgiving as we contrast it all with the anguish and despair of Mary at that moment? What should be our gladness, as we come daily and hourly to Him, and receive, instead of deserved condemnation, HIMSELF, and all the fulness of our salvation in Him? It is for us to be strong with a strength greater than that of the Magdalene that hour; for hers was a love full of darkness and distress, ours is a love which is full of joy.

III

PETER AND JOHN.

WE arrive at ver. 3, and address ourselves to consider some verbal details of the text in that verse and some verses which follow, and then to pause for reflection on their contents.

It may be noticed in passing that the Greek text before us in this neighbourhood is remarkably free from various readings—at least, from such various readings as in the least degree call for comment in such a study as this. The margin of Scrivener's Testament (for example) shrinks to a narrow compass here, giving only seven variants, none of them of the least practical moment for our purpose, through the first twelve verses of the chapter. This is a relief to the reader who is, above all things, looking for spiritual edification. Not that even the minutest details of a critical "apparatus" are to be despised or regarded with impatience from another view point; they are witnesses to the mass of material which exists for the determination of the text of the New Testament, a mass (need I say?) incomparably greater than that which survives in the case of any classical author. Still, it is not unwelcome to find that our examination of some passage of peculiar sanctity and glory need not be interrupted by the note which registers some *itacism*, or the presence or absence of a *subscript iota*, or the like.

Verse 3. *So Peter went out* (ἐξῆλθε). That is, he left the house where he was lodging; or he left the city gate; or the word very naturally includes both. The gates of Jerusalem were not shut, apparently, at the time. The Master and His followers had found no difficulty in leaving the city on the night of Thursday, though undoubtedly it was late when they walked to Gethsemane. The vast concourse of the Passover necessitated such laxity.

If ἐξῆλθεν includes a reference to *the house*, that house very probably was the Passover abode of St John. Not that it would be a house of his own; that would be a possession most unlikely in the case of a Galilean countryman. But St John's connexion with Jerusalem had something special in it; he was "known" (γνωστός) to the High Priest (xviii. 15), and it is at least very possible that near kindred of his were domiciled at Jerusalem, and that, if so, he lodged with them on his visits there.

So Peter and his friend *went out*, and now *they were coming to the tomb* (ἤρχοντο εἰς τὸ μνημεῖον). The Greek tense and preposition indicate that they were on the way, and now nearly there—not merely in a direction to reach the place, but almost arrived. They had left the northern gate, and were perhaps not a hundred yards on the road from that "green hill" which to us is "far away," but close to which was the Arimathean Councillor's garden wall.

Verse 4. *So they were running, the two together* ("Ετρεχον). Either they had been going at full speed all the way, or the nearness of what they craved to see now quickened their pace; but the former alternative is more likely. And now, near the goal, the other disciple προέδραμε, ran in advance, took a start forward (we observe the aorist, of course) *quicker than Peter.* He does not give the reason why, though he of all men knew. "Because he was the younger man" is an account sometimes given; but we know nothing at all of the ages of the Apostles relatively to one another. Tradition and pictures commonly make St Peter an elderly man beside the Lord Jesus and beside St John; but it is at least as likely that the company were much of an age with one another and with their blessed Leader. In xxi. 18, if I read aright the bearing of the words there, "when thou *wast young*,"[1] Peter is regarded by his Master as a young man still. But did not the feet of Peter flag because his heart was heavy and his conscience heavy-laden? It was less easy for him than for John to hasten to that tomb to which he had, so it might have seemed to his troubled soul, almost betrayed his Lord. However this might be, John did outrun his friend, *and came first to the tomb* —to the scene which still, no doubt, bore traces of the presence and then of the flight of the sentinels, who not very long before, perhaps not an hour before, had been so sorely scared by the rocking of the ground and by the Angel's glory, and had rushed in confusion into the sleeping town. All was silence now. And now *stooping from the side* (παρακύψας), *he sees lying the linen cloths.*

Such a *sideway* stooping is implied by the structure of the sepulchre. It would be the only way of looking into a horizontal cavity, through a low orifice, without so placing the body as to get in the observer's own light. As it was, he

[1] See below, p. 190.

got a view of the interior, and this was what he saw, in the twilight of the cell, doubly dusky in the early morning shadows : τὰ ὀθόνια κείμενα, the long folds, or strips, of fine white linen (ὀθόνη) lying in the grave-niche. This was not what should have been had the sacred Body been still there. *Then* he would have seen a solid white mass, an ample roll ; *now* he found a length of laid-off linens, thin and empty. And here of course was part of the mystery and surprise : the Body was gone, but the winding-sheet was left ! Of this Mary had said nothing ; her eyes and mind had observed only the removal of the stone, and her account would prepare them to find merely a vacant grave. So it was an unlooked-for riddle to explain what was there, as well as what was gone ; and with that sight and its perplexity there stole perhaps the first subtle ray of Resurrection hope into the mind of John. It was indeed a disappearance, but not a mere disappearance—certainly no hurried " snatching " of the elaborately enfolded Corpse. The long, long linens had been disengaged completely, and left in the place where what they held had been.

He did not go in, however. Why not ? There is not much need to ask any one who has ever looked into, or even upon, the coffin which conceals a beloved form, or has visited the recent grave which has received that coffin. No commentary is wanted by such readers to explain St John's look, yet refusal to step, into the tomb of his lost dear Lord and Friend. But with that simple reason of the bereaved heart others no doubt mingled. John was in a conflict now of grief *and wonder,* and thought as well as sorrow may have preoccupied him and left him motionless for the moment. But however, he *says* nothing about his reasons, and how can we analyse them all? Very subtle is the influence of character on circumstance; we should need to know John's character and Peter's far better than even we do to be able quite to tell what checked the one and what impelled the other at that narrow door. But none the less important is it to take note of these unexplained details, just because they are unexplained. Coming one after another as they do, set down thus so simply and without anxiety, yet minutely, they carry the very tone and accent of the eyewitness. We seem to stand there watching; the whole motion of the scene is before us; all is near, real, natural, visible. And then we remember that this Fourth Gospel (whoever wrote it) is no piece of modern literature, written in our age, when imagination has trained itself, more or less consciously, into an almost morbid activity, not least in the way of reconstructive narrative. It is the work of a far simpler and less self-conscious age, written (as we remarked in a previous chapter) centuries before the art of successful imitation of fact in fiction had developed itself, even in the centres of human culture. This quiet, while emphatic, minuteness of detail in a scene which yet the writer regards as vastly important would be, if I judge in the least aright, a literary impossibility in the first or second century, even for a trained *littérateur* —if the writing were not a record of observed fact. As it is, it is just the diction of him who knows that "that which our eyes have seen, and our hands have handled, concerning the Word of the Life, *that* we declare unto you" (1 John i. 1, 3); declaring it for a reason which lifts a narrator to a very different moral level from that of calculated fiction—"that your joy may be full; that ye may believe that this Jesus is the Christ, and that, believing, ye may have life in His Name."

Verse 6. *So Simon Peter comes, following him, and went into the tomb.* Perhaps only a few minutes or even moments intervened. The backward Apostle cannot have been far behind his friend, who probably, as we saw, had run in front only when both were near the garden.

And now, at once, Peter stoops and enters. Again we conjecture the motive. Why did he pass in, and leave John at the door outside? There was something characteristic in the motive, for we remember the parallel action, xxi. 7, where Peter is the disciple to hurry to the shore. In this case was not the heart whose intensity of emotion checked the feet on the way, just the heart to find itself unable to linger a moment when the feet had reached the goal? However this may be, here again is the touch of historical, not poetic or constructive, detail.

And he views the linen cloths lying. He takes his view, he gazes : θεωρεῖ, far more than βλέπει (ver. 5), means a deliberate look—the look of one who is taking in the scene and something of its significance. And what does he say about it? For indeed we seem to hear him speaking from within the cavern, and telling his friend outside, point by point, what he finds : "Yes, here are the winding-sheets as you saw them; and here, too, what you did not see, is the napkin, the *sudarium*, which was fastened round His head. It is put here, or left here, apart, by itself; not thrown on the rest, but rolled up (ἐντετυλιγμένον), in a separate place (εἰς ἕνα τόπον[1])." *He views the linen cloths lying, and the napkin that was over His head, not lying with the linen cloths, but apart, rolled up and put in a separate place.*

Here were fresh signs of something very different from what they and Mary had feared. Here was no hostile invasion of the grave, no rough and careless removal; rather all the marks of order and attention, we might almost say of neatness. If, in that moment of profound feeling, there was time to think (and thought often goes quickest at such times), John might have thought how entirely unlike this was to the work of enemies, and that to remove the Body at all was extremely unlike the work of friends. Who would have done it? Joseph of Arimathea—the very man who had laid the shrouded Body there with such reverent pains? Any other members of the circle of disciples or supporters? Such a thought as this last most certainly would not have occurred to John, in the entire absence of probable motive. All alike were unexpectant of a Resurrection; all alike were in the depth of distress and disappointment, and probably also in much alarm for their own safety. All, if they had leisure or

---

[1] Literally, of course, "*into* one place"; brought to it and laid *in* it.

courage for much such reflection, must have been thankful that their beloved Master had found (by no means of theirs, for they had none) an honourable burial. Certainly, in any case, *they* would not have stripped the cloths away.

Enemies had not so gently unwound the corpse. Friends would not have unwound it at all.

Verse 8. So, with the dawn of a blissful hope in his soul, and probably with a sudden throng of memories in his mind—memories of words spoken by Jesus, and of prophecies He had half explained—*the other disciple, who came first to the tomb, went in.*

And he saw (εἶδε). Here is a third verb, with βλέπειν and θεωρεῖν. And it is used in its proper place: ἰδεῖν tends to indicate a sight which is also intelligence. He saw the facts and their meaning.

And believed. Here was infinitely more than an empty grave, an absent corpse, an unused winding-sheet, a folded napkin. Here was— Resurrection. He believed, he accepted without direct sight the certainty, that there was life here, after death. He believed the *fact* that Jesus lived again, and he believed the *truth;* he recognized a *divine* fact, a fact of prophecy. For how does he proceed?

Verse 9. *For not as yet did they know the Scripture, that of necessity He would rise from the dead;* that by a supreme necessity, in the predestination of the eternal plan of Messiah's work, He would die and rise again.

The Scripture (τὴν γραφήν) : a singular which seems almost always in the New Testament to refer to some one *passage* of the Old. We are not told what "Scripture" to St John just then shone out as *the* Resurrection promise; but as we read the Pentecostal Sermon of his friend (Acts ii.), we may well suppose that Psalm xvi. may have been the place.[1] But whatever "the Scripture" was, "they" had not understood it. But now John—at least John —did. The ray of fulfilment lighted up the prophecy. The fact, once seen, began at once to kindle into the glorious truth. The grave was vacant, and so vacant that it was plain that Jesus had not been lifted away from it by other hands; He had *left* it. And so at once the strangely-hidden secret was solved; the impossible, the incredible, the unwelcome had become

[1] The "Scripture" for a *third-day* resurrection is undoubtedly, on our Lord's own testimony, the narrative of Jonah. But the third day is not immediately in view here.—The testimony of this brief passage to the apostolic belief in definitely predictive prophecy is very impressive, by its very passingness.

the glorious truth of life. Jesus, the Dead, was risen.

He believed—with a faith decisive and new, as an experience in his mind. What a wonderful candour there is in the admission, "as yet they did not know"! This aged saint and prophet does not shrink from telling the world that for three long years, spent in his Saviour's company, he had laboured under an immense mistake about that Saviour's work. He had laid his head upon the breast of Jesus Christ, and yet had never understood that He had come on purpose to die and to rise again. This is no ordinary frankness; it is, in fact, nothing less than the simplicity of transparent truth, the truthfulness of a man to whom the reality, the glory, the blessedness of his Master are so precious that he cannot pause a moment to think of his own reputation in telling his Master's story. Rather, he is glad to recall the contrast, because it was even more happy than humbling —the contrast between his own strange blindness in the old days and the sunrise of joy and life upon which he now entered, and which he owed entirely to his Lord. We are welcome to know anything, everything, about John's slowness, dulness, oblivion, ignorance, about his poor insight into Scripture, his earthly view of the

Kingdom, his temporal ambition, his unbelieving despair, if the contrast may only lead us, for whom he writes, and whom he loves by anticipation as fellow-believers, to a full view of the sacrifice, the victory, the life, the love of the Lord Jesus Christ. "He knoweth that he saith true, that ye might believe."

So, with all the quiet simplicity of truth, he closes this part of the story. Ver. 10: *So the disciples went away again to their own abode* (πρὸς ἑαυτούς). That was all—all, at least, that we are to know for the present. We have seen them in the moment of their first faith long enough to confirm our faith; but how they felt, what they said, on the way home, and at home, what Peter said to John about the denial in this new light, and what John said to Peter, what Mary felt and said when they met her beneath the roof of John's abode—all this we do not know. It is all written, not for effect, but for fact; for truth, for faith, that we too might believe.

For my own part, after tracing out again the details of this section of St John's story, one thought comes uppermost in the mind—the thought how invaluable to the enquirer after Jesus Christ, and also, at least as much, to the believer in Him, are the strong, definite lines of *the narrative* of His triumph. Here we have been standing almost entirely aside from explicit Christian doctrine, and looking simply at events. Some of them have been very small events in themselves: the grief and hurry of one affectionate woman; the actions of curiosity and search on the part of two perplexed and anxious men; and then the fact that they had mistaken certain venerable writings; and then their quiet retirement to their abode again. No instruction; all narrative.

For that very reason, how invaluable it is in its proper place! How good it is for me, for many reasons, for reasons the very deepest, to be able to touch this paragraph, and handle it, and feel in it the texture of mere fact; to find myself in contact, not with a poetic cloud, however coloured, but with the angles of the Rock of Ages! The material is hard, for it is solid; hard with a hardness which sustains, not wounds. It is the rock; it is indissoluble fact. I take no pains to make it stronger; I neither can nor need; it is *fait accompli;* Jesus is risen.

Why is this fact-character of the Gospel so very valuable to me? this objectivity, this view of spiritual truth as bound up for ever with events which really happened in time and place, quite external to me and independent of me?

It is so because, on the other hand, my need of the Gospel is a thing so deeply *internal*. I know, with the most direct of all sorts of knowledge, I know as an inner fact, my essential need of a SAVIOUR. I know my sin, and I know my want. There is that in me which asks, and must ask till satisfied, for pardon and for holiness. And this asking is prompted by more motives than one. First, as regards the question of pardon, there is the conviction (very definite, stern, and unpoetical) that without pardon there is danger, danger of an indefinitely awful sequel to the fact of unforgiven sin. And then, in a similar way, the desire for victory over sin, and for the liberty of holiness, arises in part from a very stern, simple source—from the fact that sin met with compromise puts a hopeless bar between me and the possession of the peace of God. And then, in harmony with these inner facts, springing up with them, yet from an even greater depth, there are other reasons. Somehow I know that I am made to know God and to love Him, and that the heart will not rest until it rests in Him.[1] It stands to reason, in the deepest sense of reason. What

---

[1] Augustine: *Confessiones, ad init.*

but the Maker Himself, to the thinking thing which He has made, can be the point of rest, the ultimate centre, the never-disappointing satisfaction, the spring never dry, the tree which bears fruit every month? Positively or negatively, the human soul is always athirst for God, for the living God. Probably we, writer and reader, have known more or less of both phases of that thirst; the negative consciousness, as we become aware of the insufficiency of anything less than Him for rest and joy; and then the positive consciousness, when grace shows us that the Lord God, known, trusted, embraced, is "all our desire," our joy which cannot waste, our pure and purifying happiness.

So the soul asks, implores, the pardon which it knows it will never merit. It asks, it thirsts, for the knowledge of the Eternal Holy and Happy One, and, in that knowledge, for a joy which is absolutely unattainable elsewhere.

Now, the very fact that these realities of the inmost heart of man are what they are, *internal* facts, is what gives its peculiar preciousness to the objectivity of the Gospel, to its character as a compact mass of *external* events, achievements, done apart from us, done for us, by Another.

When the soul cries out for God, it implores

not an echo, but an answer. A mere series of impressions roused by another series will not satisfy. No webs woven out of "inner consciousness" will bear the strain of the consciousness of conviction. No Saviour constructed out of the elements of self can be the Saviour from self, from the sentence hanging over it, from the bondage of sin within it.

Here the revelation of our Lord Jesus Christ comes in as it is. From the exactly opposite quarter it comes to meet me at the precise point of my need. It is not aspiration, or emotion. It is fact—outside, objective, the work of Another; done in history; done without thought, or choice, or leave of mine; while I was non-existent; while I was yet to be, and was foreseen as yet to be, in all my sinfulness and extreme unworthiness of such benefits. And this work of Another, what is it? It is the death and triumph of the Eternal and Incarnate Son of God.

This is history, recorded and attested event. It no more depends on me for its truth than does the history of Cæsar, or of Cromwell. External to me stands this wonderful fact, Jesus Christ, slain and risen. I do not make it, but I take it.

He is, indeed, "the thing that I long for";

the propitiation for my sin, proved to be such by His resurrection after His altar-death; the adequate Cause, wholly by Himself, why even I, touching Him, united to Him, should be not only forgiven but accepted with divine joy by the Father who infinitely loves Him.

He in His Person and Character is indeed competent to fulfil my heart's longing for a satisfying Object of pure and worshipping love—"chief among ten thousand, altogether lovely."

And this wonderful and all-blessed Lord thus satisfies the human soul because He is not the echo but the answer. He is not a splendid figment of speculation. He is revealed through events of history; in lines of fact which do not depend on our moods, and cannot change. He is revealed in a historical though supernatural birth, a historical though sinless life, a historical while propitiatory death, a historical while supremely miraculous resurrection. As He is history, He stands clear of this sinful, anxious, inner world of mine; and He is therefore able, as He is the Truth, to be its refuge and its peace. Jesus Christ, immovable in Himself, is my point of rest, my spring of life.

Such are some of the thankful thoughts with which we may stand by the empty sepulchre while the Apostles walk away to their own home. The garden, the rock, the cave, the winding-sheet, are no scene of romance; they are historical: "Handle them and see." Jesus Christ has actually suffered and risen again in anticipation of my needs, and of my complete incapacity to meet those needs out of the resources of self.

Let us often walk to Joseph's garden accordingly. When the heart is heavy and weary, casting about for peace, or when it is preoccupied and earthly, and refuses to attach itself in conscious, affectionate faith to its one and perfect hope, Jesus Christ, then let us not go deeper into the heart, for it will only disappoint us, but let us return to the facts—to the Person who is our Life. Let us stand again beside the open and vacant sepulchre, and see again and trust again the risen Son of God. There let us leave behind alike self's sinfulness and its imagined righteousness, and calmly give thanks for His great glory and accomplished work, joining Bonar as he sings:

> Thy works, not mine, O Christ,
> Speak gladness to my heart;
> They tell me all is done,
> They bid my fear depart.

IV

MARY AND THE LORD.

Our last study closed with verse 10. We watched the departure of Peter and John from the garden to the city, as they retired with the new-born belief in their hearts that Jesus was risen, while the light of prophecy broke in on that astonishing fact and turned it into a glorious truth of redemption.

How brief, how unadorned, is the notice in the narrative: *So the disciples went back to their own abode* (πρὸς ἑαυτούς). Its simplicity is one of the many notes of truth in the passage. No creator of an unreal scene (writing within the first two centuries) would have thought of sending them away so quietly, with so little apparent *effect* in the story. Such simplicity, meanwhile, is quite in the manner of the Fourth Gospel. It is of a piece with the extremely simple sequel of the raising of Lazarus, and again with the noble brevity of verse 21 below: *So the disciples were glad, seeing the Lord.*

Here the narrator is already occupied, so to speak, with the next great fact in the chain of events, the appearance to Mary. Peter and John have done their part, they have borne their witness to the Resurrection by telling us what they found in the tomb; now it is time for Mary's witness.

Once more we pause to observe the holy carelessness of the Evangelist about his own apostolic prominence, or Peter's, apart from the relation which he and Peter bear to Christ. The two leading Apostles, and their new resurrection-faith, are in his view merely a fragment of the witness to Jesus. And if the solitary woman left weeping by the empty cave can serve as well, or better, for the next fragment of that witness, let Peter and John move away unnoticed, and let Mary fill the scene.

"We preach not," and we depict not, "ourselves, but Christ Jesus as Lord, and ourselves your bondservants, because of Jesus" (2 Cor. iv. 5); such is the uniform spirit of the Apostles and Evangelists. For our little sphere, let it be always our spirit too. If we would have it so, we must be always learning their secret; we must have for ourselves the Lord Jesus as the one grand certainty, satisfaction, joy, and hope.

The quiet self-forgetfulness of St John's treatment of narrative (a spirit which appears, indeed, though in different forms, far and wide in Scripture narrations generally) is a phenomenon full of importance. Certainly it is a literary paradox, this balance, this calmness, when we remember at the same time the prodigious character of the events related. The morning of the Resurrection is described with the same simplicity and absence of effort as the conversation by Jacob's Well. How does this simple and unanxious manner tell as an inner evidence of truthfulness? Somewhat thus, if I read aright. Had the story of the Resurrection, and the whole circle of Gospel miracles, been a creation of imagination, a result merely of mental and spiritual emotion, then the emotions and impressions (to produce the results which followed) must have been very vehement experiences of highly excitable minds. And if so, if this were all, then these same minds would have been left, on the hypothesis, to work out their emotions as they might, uncontrolled, uncorrected, by the word and power of a risen Redeemer. The issue of such conditions would surely be not only hopeless divergences but wild exaggerations. But what we have as a fact before us is at least substantial consistency of statement and great calmness of manner. To any one who watches carefully the ways of man this is good moral evidence, not that nothing extraordinary had occurred, but that the wonderful something which had occurred had come with amplest warrant of its reality, and had become a permanent and most powerful, while elevating and calming, factor in the minds of the narrators.

The Evangelist writes of the Resurrection with dispassionate calmness because the Resurrection was an objective fact, absolutely certain; and because the Risen One had come back not merely to be seen and vanish, but to teach, to control, and to abide with His disciples' souls for ever.

This same quietness of manner, with the same explanation, may be traced back into the narratives of the Crucifixion-time, where the Evangelists display an altogether wonderful calmness and (if I may use the word) fairness of tone in describing the conduct of the enemies and murderers of their Lord.

But it is more than time to proceed in our study of the text, from verse 11 and onwards.

But Mary was standing at the tomb, weeping, outside. So while she wept, she stooped from the side (to look) into the tomb, and beholds (θεωρεῖ) *two angels, in white, seated, one at the head and one at the feet, where lay the body of Jesus. And they say to her, Woman, why do you weep? She says to them, Because they have taken away my Lord, and I do not know where they have put Him. And with these words she turned backwards, and beholds Jesus, standing, and did not know that it was Jesus. Jesus says to her, Woman, why do you weep? whom do you seek? She, thinking that it is the gardener, says to Him, Sir, if you carried Him off, tell me where you put Him, and I will take Him away. Jesus says to her, Mary! Turning, she says to Him, Rabbouni, which means, Master (Διδάσκαλε). Jesus says to her, Do not touch (feel) Me, for I have not yet gone up to My Father. Go to My brethren, and say to them, I go up to My Father and your Father, and My God and your God. Mary of Magdala comes, reporting to the disciples that she has seen the Lord, and that He said these things to her.*

Verse 11. *But Mary was standing at the tomb.* Εἰστήκει, she had taken her place, and was now there. Probably she had followed the Apostles out from the city, but more slowly. She would be left behind naturally by the pace of the two eager men, young as probably they both were; and besides, she would hurry less, as she knew the fact, which they had yet to assure themselves of, that the tomb was empty. She entered the garden after them, perhaps unnoticed by them, and not much heeding their looks and words as they entered successively and saw what the cavern had to reveal. We need not wonder at the absorbed unconsciousness of one another which those disciples, men and women, showed that morning. After all these Christian centuries, and after our personal Christian education, it is hard for us, even when we have found the Saviour with joy for our own, to realize what was the first grief for His death and the first joy for His resurrection. Those were moments which to an unknown degree threw minds and hearts back on themselves.

So, for the time, Mary was to the Apostles, and they were to her, as if they were not. Was Jesus stolen away? was Jesus risen again?—that was all.

The loving and desolate Galilean woman remains, then, as she thinks, all alone. If she just noticed the silent departure of Peter and John, it only said to her the worst—the Lord was not in the tomb, the Lord's body was gone. So she "stood," seemingly as if paralysed: not kneeling, making no gesture of misery; standing, just as she had come, κλαίουσα, weeping, alone. And yet, like other sorrowful disciples since, she was not alone. Angels were just in front of her, and the Lord was just behind her. And the very thing which caused her tears, His absence from the place where she sought Him, was soon to be her blessed surprise, her sudden and endless joy.

So *Mary was standing, at the tomb, weeping, outside.* Thus the words follow each other in the Greek.

Verse 12. *So while she wept, she stooped from the side to look into the tomb, and beholds two angels, in white, seated, one at the head and one at the feet, where the body of Jesus lay.*

Again detail follows detail with a peculiar and thrilling simplicity. While weeping, she bent her head and looked in; the look not of curiosity, but of bereaved love, which in a sad unreasoning way cares for the bare spot where the beloved has been. And now her wet eyes, gazing fixedly (θεωρεῖ), see two human figures in the dark place; for simply human in form, surely, all Angels are in Scripture when they appear in intercourse with men; the winged aspect is seen only in symbolic or mystic surroundings. There they are, two youthful watchers, as we may suppose them to look (Mark xvi. 5, νεανίσκοι), seated, in quiet dignity, one at each end of the niche in the cavern-wall, where the holy Body had lain in its linen folds. They were ἐν λευκοῖς, in white clothing, white and more than white, positively bright[1]; so we gather from Luke xxiv. 4, ἐν ἐσθήσεσιν ἀστραπτούσαις. We may compare the word στίλβειν used for the white raiment of the transfigured Lord Himself, Mark ix. 3. Such a radiance, or something like it, shone in that garden sepulchre, touching with light its rocky roof, and walls, and floor, and "the linen cloths" as they lay there. There, before this weeping disciple, this once possessed and miserable woman, sat revealed those two inhabitants of the heavenly home. And listen; to reassure her, to tell her that it is no delusion generated by her glancing tears, they speak to her, perhaps one by one, in human words, and with gentle, I might almost say respectful, sympathy: *Woman, why do you weep?* Γύναι, as all know, is a word of perfect courtesy, a word of as much possible respectfulness as Κύριε would be in an address to a man. *Woman, lady, why do you weep?*

It is a moving thing to observe the sympathy of Angels with men and women, as Scripture so very often brings it out. "These things" (the

---

[1] See Trench on the word λευκός in his commentary on Rev. ii. 17.

salvation of sinners by the Son of God) "Angels desire to look into" (1 Pet. i. 12); and indeed we find it to be so with them whenever the veil is lifted. They are no mere official dignitaries of the court of heaven, just stooping to hand a message of reprieve to pardoned rebels of an alien race. They come as brethren to brethren, as servants to fellow-servants, as lovers and worshippers of the Son of God to those who, in the midst of sin and death, yet love and worship Him also. Aye, they come as to those whose nature He has taken, and who do not grudge sinful man that inexplicable and inexpressible privilege, but love him for it. So Mary, this weeping child of a sinful race, all weakness, all mistake, is to these heavenly ones an object of holy sympathy. To them she is one whom Jesus Christ loves, and who loves Him, and it is enough. *Why do you weep? Whom do you seek?*

Verse 13. But for Mary all this is, for the present, nothing. In her then state of thought and feeling, the appearances and the voices were to her as things of every day, commonplace, indifferent. She just answers, *Because they have taken away my Lord, and I do not know where they have put Him.*

Nothing could be more curiously truth-like

and truthful than this indifference of Mary of Magdala. It was quite another thing than the startled *fear* of the women when (Matt. xxviii. 5, 8) the Angel appeared on the stone. That was a shock, a sudden sight, on their first arrival. Here grief had had time to deepen, and to fix itself on the absorbing fact of the absence of Jesus. And such was the bitterness of that absence of the Body which (to her mind at that time) was so soon to be dust—such was the grief of its absence, because He was her Lord, that the sight of two Angels, and their audible voices, were to her, wonderfully yet naturally, as nothing.

What would it be to us if our Lord, as we have learnt to know Him, were removed? What if Jesus were found absent from our heart, our life, our earth, our heaven? If He—not the slain, but the slain and living, Lamb of God, our Lord, were found to be non-existent, or existent no more for us? Would not our souls so fail as to find no rest, no remedy anywhere else? Should we not really feel that heaven itself and its inhabitants, without Him (*per impossibile*), would be blank, unsatisfying, even formidable? Yes, for heaven is not the cause of our pardon, nor the source of our life, nor is the angelic race our Saviour and King.

And if indeed He is, as He is, such that nothing can ever possibly take His place for us, what a place should His be in the heart! Henceforth we will more than ever watch and pray against even the transient pain, so heavy and so paralysing, of even seeming to find Him absent, sin having taken away our Lord, and we know not where He is gone.

Verse 14. *And with these words she turned backwards, and beholds* (θεωρεῖ) *Jesus, standing, and did not know that it is Jesus.*

She turned backwards, bent her stooping head towards the garden, not the cavern. It is vain perhaps to ask what made her turn. Chrysostom gives a singularly beautiful explanation—that, as the Lord appeared, the Angels did obeisance, and Mary turned to see *to whom*. Or, as some have guessed, she felt that subtle consciousness of some one near her which we have all probably felt at times. But was it not simply the aimless movement of a new disappointment? The long look into the cave has told her that Jesus is not there, and now she will look away, and go away.

St John, we may be sure, is here recording exactly what Mary told him. "So I turned my head, and there behind me stood, as I thought, the gardener."

And she sees Jesus, standing. The word θεωρεῖ is again used. Even here, though certainly at first sight it is less easy to read than usual, we do read its distinctive meaning, the "seeing" of a deliberate gaze.[1] The look she gave was but sidelong, for see below, ver. 16, where she "turns herself" again more completely. But it was steady. She deliberately and distinctly saw some one there.

Whence the Lord had come we do not know. How long He had been there, whether up to that moment He had been visible to any one, whether He now appeared in His familiar form, we are not told. But He was there, none the less because Mary did not know Him and so little realized all that He was.

There stood the Lord of death and life, fresh from bearing that disciple's sins and ours, from those unfathomable and unknown sorrows of His Soul (ἄγνωστα παθήματα) which went to make the ransom of our souls; just come from the unseen world "in the power of an indissoluble life" (Heb. vii. 16). There He stood before her. And He was "the same Jesus" still; the same in corporeal and spiritual iden-

---

[1] See this meaning at once unmistakable, and spiritually most important, in John vi. 40.

tity, the very Body which had been torn by the Roman scourges and nails, the very Soul which had been exceeding sorrowful unto death; the same Humanity under the same Personality, glorified but identical. And He was the same too in moral identity, the unalterable Lord Jesus in faithfulness, patience, and love. He dies for His doubting and mistaking followers; He rises for them, and finds them mistaking and despairing. They, if I may say so, are still themselves, and more than themselves, in their imperfections; He is still Himself, and more than Himself, in His perfections. He is about to deal with Mary, and with the two, and the ten, and Thomas, as indeed "this same Jesus"; so we shall see in due time. There is strong consolation in this picture of the moral identity of the risen Lord.

But she did not know that it is Jesus. Though essentially the same, He was to her now different. Partly, no doubt, it was simply a case of imperfect sight. She did not see Him full; perhaps she did not look *in His face* at all; and she was in tears. But also we have here, surely, one of the many cases (Matt. xxviii. 17; Mark xvi. 13; Luke xxiv. 16, 37; John xxi. 4) where we trace a change in the aspect of the Risen Saviour, and also that it was His pleasure sometimes not to be recognized, checking the message of the eyes to the mind.

In passing I see here again an evidence of truth. A fabricated narrative would hardly have gone out of its way to say that the Risen One, after forty hours' absence, was at first not recognized. It might even seem suspicious, were it not true. *All* the Gospels record this inability of the disciples to recognize their Lord at once, and then go on to show how fully the doubt was removed. And how *permanently* it was removed! After Thomas' recovery to faith we detect in the first age of Christianity no trace of the least hesitancy, no whisper of a word of retractation of certainty, on the part of any one of the professed witnesses of the Resurrection. No heretic, no pagan, has preserved the faintest tradition of any after misgiving in the Church of the witnesses.

Verse 15. *Jesus says to her, Woman, why do you weep? whom do you seek?*[1] Blessed enquiries, from that Enquirer. When Jesus Christ asks us about our sorrows their truest comfort is already begun; when He asks about

---

[1] "This first word of the Risen Lord to a mortal is an inexhaustible text for the Resurrection, which it is the business of the preacher to unfold. He has risen again to comfort those who mourn" (Stier).

our loss, our blank, He has already begun to fill it. Happy those who, like Mary, are found by Him, even if they are found grieving for Him and missing Him. We must not fear to tell Him all our fears. There is sure to be some element of sin, however recondite, in them. There was such an element in Mary's fears; she *ought* to have remembered His many promises better, and trusted them more firmly. She *ought* to have known that, come what might, He must conquer and reign. Yes, even a Mary at the tomb had sin somewhere in her unhopefulness. Yet the Risen Lord came in person to dispel it. And to us He is ready to come as personally to help us, not because we deserve, but because we need; because in our guilty weakness we are so disappointing, if the word may be allowed, to Him. So we will come, and speak out, keeping nothing back, telling Him our worst misgiving, as simply as if we could hear Him say, "Why do you weep? What do you want?"

But Mary is slow to see the light of joy. Perhaps already she has turned her eyes away again. She is so little conscious of supernatural glories and joys close to her that she thinks she sees there—Joseph's gardener! A very homely, unsentimental conjecture it was; certainly not the thought of a *femme hallucinée* such as Renan, himself hallucinated, supposes her to have been. She was quite sane, though very sad, when she said to herself, "It is the gardener." In great sorrow there is sometimes a cool, prosaic consciousness of trifling or common things around, as curious as it is real; the high wrought state of the mind leaves it open more than usual to the touch of even small impressions. So Mary would seem rapidly to have *calculated*, "It is the rich man's gardener; the Sabbath is past, and they may work. Joseph did not intend my Master's Body to stay permanently in his fine grave, only to rest there for a while, because it was so near; and now his servant has been told to take the Body away and bury it somewhere else." And then, with the resolve of a love which felt as if it could move mountains, she thinks she will take it into her own care, lift it, carry it, bestow it in some untroubled sepulchre, if she may but have it again. *Sir*, so the helpless mourner speaks, with the deference of helplessness, *if you carried Him off, tell me where you put Him, and I will take Him away.*

"*Him:*"—she uses no name; no need to do so occurs to her. Jesus, even slain and gone, fills her whole thought, and she assumes that it must be so with others too.

How truth-like again in every detail! the submissive sadness of the appeal, and, on the other hand, the blind energy of love, which undertakes, in the exhaustion of grief, to do the work of a strong man, removing and burying the Body.

So she plans a second interment for Jesus, while the living Jesus is there, and just about to lift her in the embrace of His manifested power and love.

Verse 16. *Jesus says to her, Mary!* The reading Μαριάμ, *Miriam*, is, on the whole, most probable here; the specially Jewish form of the name, not *Maria*, its Greek equivalent. It is interesting to remember that the same Voice, at a later day, spoke to another heart by its own home-name, Σαούλ, not Σαῦλε (so in all the narratives of the great Conversion). It is observable, whatever inferences we may draw, that where the Evangelists record the Lord's utterance of an Aramaic word or sentence the occasion is almost always one where a specially close and personal appeal was needed. The Aramaic of the cry from the Cross is scarcely an exception.[1]

[1] See this handled very ably in Dr Alex. Roberts' *Discussions on the Gospels*.

But this is a minor point here; the all-important fact here is that He used the woman's *name*. The personal appeal, the voice to the individual, to that mysterious personality with which, as a fact, man so intimately connects his *name*—it is this we are to notice. It is no longer *Woman*, it is *Mary*. Any voice might have said the first; the speaker of this last, then and there, must be no other than the Friend who had set her free.

Turning, she says to Him, Rabboni, or more precisely, probably, (some think that we have here a *Galilean* form,) *Rabbouni*. This St John at once explains; *which means Master*, Διδάσκαλε, *Teacher;* but, of course, with the conveyed idea (in the Hebrew) of the greatness, the venerability, of the Teacher. The termination, it would seem (Rabboun*i*), may either be the possessive suffix (*My* Master), or an appellative (*O* Master); either alternative gives much the same impression of intensity and reverent endearment. With the word, she clasps Him as He stands. In that tumult of fear, love, and joy, to assure herself of the objective reality of His presence, she lays her touch, the touch which *feels* (ἅπτομαι), on His sacred Person, probably on the feet, towards which she bent. Compare Matt. xxviii. 9.

MARY AND THE LORD.

Verse 17. *Jesus says to her, Do not touch (feel) Me, for I have not yet gone up to My Father. Go to My brethren, and say to them, I go up to My Father and your Father, and My God and your God. Mary of Magdala comes reporting to the disciples that she has seen the Lord, and that He said these things to her.*

The two verses, 17, 18, I thus merely translate. It would be impossible in this chapter to dwell on ver. 17, with its problems of reference, and its depth of truth about the Father, the Son, and the soul.

Let us for the present close with the delightful effort to place ourselves in thought beside those two persons, in the calm, silent morning of that wonderful spring-time, in Joseph's garden. Looking on them we forget, as the Gospel forgets, the blessed Angels close at hand; JESUS and Mary Magdalene have much more to do than they with our salvation and peace. It is indeed a place good to visit, and to visit at the moment we have studied. We stand upon the common earth; the ground of a garden, near the walls of a still existing town, a garden whose last traces are, some think, still visible. We see the cavern tomb, and its round door-stone rolled out. We look up to the common morning sky, through the garden trees. But in that quiet place and hour JESUS Himself is making known, for the very first time, the success, the completeness, the glory of His salvation. It is HE who stands literally there, speaking to Mary, but now much more speaking to us, to you, to me, as we too "turn" to Him to hear His words about Himself. He points *us* to His own open grave; that is, to His accomplished victory for us, His finished atonement for our sins. He points us to His living Self, living immortally, eternally, living at this moment, and present with us, even when "we perceive Him not." He points us to the heavens above, and tells us that He is going thither, and that we, for whom He has died, and who have come to Him, and whose sins—including doubts and fears—He has wonderfully cancelled in His own blood, may be sure that for us that heaven is home. It is home for Peter, who denied Him; for the Eleven, who forsook Him; for Magdalene, who thought that His death was the end. It is home for us, unworthy; for He is there. Henceforth, the earth and the heavens are filled for us with light—the light of the redemption, the love, and the presence, of the sacrificed and risen Son of God.

V

FROM THE GARDEN TO THE CHAMBER.

Our last study brought us to the close of the account of the interview of Mary Magdalene with the Risen Lord. In a passage so conspicuously rich in treasures of grace and truth, I make no apology for leaving some points quite untouched. But on two main points, which have been touched in some sort, so little has been said that some additional words must be said upon them now, and at more length.

I refer to two topics given us by the utterance of the Lord Jesus in ver. 17: *Do not touch Me, for I have not yet gone up to My Father. Go to My brethren, and say to them, I go up to My Father and your Father, and My God and your God.*

(i.) The prohibition and command to Mary. I need not explain to my readers what difficulty this has presented to expositors. What was the touching? Why was it forbidden? What was the connexion (observe the "*for*") between the "Touch Me not" and the "I have not yet gone up to My Father"? These questions have been very variously answered.

Yet we may be sure that the first meaning, however, must have been intended to be quite simple. Addressed to that loving disciple, in that moment of supreme emotion, the logic cannot have been recondite or involved, in the blessed Speaker's purpose. In view of this, I incline to that explanation of the passage which connects as closely as possible the prohibition "Touch Me not" with the commission "Go to My brethren." We observe that the Greek verb is in the present, or continuing, imperative, not in the aorist subjunctive; μή μου ἅπτου, not μή μου ἅψῃ. Accordingly, by familiar laws of Greek usage, it conveys an order not to forbear touching Him at all, but to forbear a longer, a prolonged, touching. She is not to linger over it: it is enough; let her remove the hand which *feels* the sacred limb.

The verb ἅπτομαι occurs only here in St John. But its general usage assures us that it indicates here nothing like clasping or clinging, as when the women (Matt. xxviii. 9) "held Him by the feet." It means no more than simple touching. It occurs, for example, where the Lord (Mark

viii. 22) is asked to "touch" a blind man's eyes; and where the suffering woman (Matt. ix. 21) plans to "touch" just the fringe of His garment. Here Mary Magdalene may have just laid her hand, in felt contact and no more, on His foot, or on His hand; not clinging, not embracing, only *feeling*, as if to make certain that no vision, but the living LORD, was there. And it is this then which He thus gently checked. We cannot see in the prohibition accordingly anything like a reproof, as if she had taken a liberty, as if she had not been reverent enough. The thoughts familiarly associated with *Noli me tangere*, as a quoted phrase, are quite out of place here.

May we not paraphrase the purport of the words of Jesus somewhat thus? "Do not linger here, touching Me, to ascertain My bodily reality, in the incredulity of your exceeding joy. I *am* in very fact before you, standing quite literally and locally on this plot of ground, not yet ascended to the heavens; you need not doubt, and ask, and test. And, moreover, there is another reason why not to linger thus; I have an errand for you, Mary. I desire you to go hence, and at once, for Me; to go to My brethren, and to tell them that I *am* about to go up thither; that in glorious fact I am risen, and therefore on My way to the throne; going to My Father and their Father, and My God and their God."

She might be sure that He was literally, and still, on earth; so she need not any longer touch Him. She was to carry the tidings to the disciples; so she must not any longer linger at His side.

Here then we may further trace, with thanksgiving, a lesson for all believers, for all and sundry who (Rom. x. 9; Heb. xiii. 20) "believe in the heart that the God of peace hath brought again from the dead our Lord Jesus, that great Shepherd of the sheep." The lesson is, not to be too constantly and too anxiously tracing and retracing the evidence of the glorious fact of the Resurrection, vitally precious as that evidence is, and not to stay pondering and enjoying that fact for one's self only, and so, inevitably, with an imperfect realization; but to carry on to others the light and blessedness of the fact, of the truth, that He is "risen indeed," and ascended too; saying to them (as He shall give occasion to the glad and ready messenger) both with lips and yet more with a life full of His resurrection-life: "I have seen the Lord; He is risen, He is ascended, and our life is hid with Him in God."

Beautiful it is to observe, in the Gospel narratives of Easter, this instant commission to *all* the newly-enlightened disciples to tell to the rest, "as they mourned and wept," their glorious cause of joy, in simplicity, confidence, and love.

(ii.) And now *what was* the message which Mary was to carry, and for which she was thus to leave the tangible presence of her risen Lord? Strange to say, it is the message of His approaching departure. Not "I am come back," but "I am going away, I am going up."

Here is indeed a deeply spiritual aspect of the resurrection message. The return of the Lord Jesus bodily for a season to His people on earth, was much, unspeakably much, but it was not all; the Resurrection was the avenue to the Ascension. Or, to put it otherwise and perhaps in a safer way, as the blessed Death is seen in its comfort and glory only in the light of the Resurrection, so the Resurrection is fully seen in all its precious import only in the light of the Ascension. The Risen One is hastening on to His true place, the place of Rev. v. (where we are permitted to see the Ascension, as it were, from its heavenly side); He is going to be the Lamb *upon the throne*. The finished work of His Death and Rising, what was it but the beginning of His continuing work of Intercession? Let us not forget this in all our daily contemplation of, and intercourse with, our Lord; in our life in and on Him, who is at once our pardon, our power, and our holiness. After all, we are not so much to look back, as to look up, on Him who was crucified for us and rose again. His atonement is in one supreme aspect absolute, complete, never to be repeated. We rest on it as on "fact accomplished." We know that He did once, and now no more for ever, bear for us the unknown burthen of our guilt. But the application of His atonement, in some of its most precious aspects, is a thing incessant. Momentarily needed (for sin's prevention as well as cure), it is momentarily applied to the believer's soul; it is free and efficacious each day, and hour, and moment, for our reception, and possession, and enjoyment:

> His love intense, His merit fresh,
> As if but newly slain.

Our safety under that Shelter, once given in covenant, is ever being given in actual mercy and truth; and so too is our fruition of the once-pledged gift of His Holy Spirit, that gift so vitally connected (see Gal. iii. 13, 14) with our justification through the merits of the Crucified Jesus. And how do we joyfully know that this giving *is* thus continuous? We know it because Jesus Christ is not only risen, but ascended also. "It is Christ that died, yea, rather, that is risen again, who is even at the right hand of God, who also maketh intercession for us." "He, by the right hand of God exalted, hath shed forth this" (Rom. viii. 34; Acts ii. 33).

The Epistle to the Hebrews, in its great picture of the Lord Jesus as the true High Priest, emphasizes this in a very remarkable way. The Death, the precious blood, is everywhere in the Epistle; but we read of the Resurrection only once (xiii. 20). The Resurrection, in the main argument, is merged in the Ascension; and this because the intercession of our Aaron-Melchisedec is essentially bound up with His Ascension. He intercedes "for ever" as "a Priest upon *His throne*." "When He had by Himself purged our sins, He *sat down* on the right hand of the Majesty on high" (i. 3; see iv. 14; vi. 20; vii. 25, 26; viii. 1; ix. 11, 12, 24; x. 12, 13; xii. 2, 24).

Thus the Ascension is, in deepest spiritual truth, the sum and crown of the work of Jesus Christ. Looking at it through the lens of Scripture, we see, gathered into one, the rays of the Cross and of the Resurrection, the atoning Work once and for ever done, and the ceaseless

Result, in the power of the Lord's endless life, ever flowing out, flowing down, from Him who, as our Mediator and as our Head, ever liveth to make intercession for us; to receive for us, to give to us.

Thus, although that very evening He is going to visit His brethren, and to fill them with the mingled natural and spiritual joys of His Resurrection, He sends on to them in advance the message of the coming joy, greater and wholly spiritual, of His Ascension. And note well the terms of the message: it is an Ascension not merely to heaven, but to a God and Father. And to what a God, what a Father! No mere Absolute or Supreme, no mere First Cause, unknown perhaps, and unknowable, except as an antecedent Somewhat demanded by the logic of phenomena. Jesus Christ is going into the depths of the unseen universe; yet whither He goes we know, for we know to Whom He goes. We have a double, nay, a quadruple description of HIM, to fix and to fill our thought. HE is Father, and He is God, each in two respects; first, in each case, in relation to Jesus Christ, then, in relation to His brethren. Here is a fourfold chain of truth, light, and love by which the believing sinner, coming to the sinner's Friend, lays hold of nothing less than the throne and of Him who sits thereon.

We observe, of course, and we have all done so a hundred times, the fact that the chain *is* not double but quadruple : not "our Father and our God" (the Lord Jesus never speaks so ; His nearest approach to it, and that is not really the same thing, occurs John iv. 22 : "*we* know what *we worship*") but "Mine and yours" in each case. It is the same relation, but predicated in different respects, when the Saviour and the disciple are respectively in view. Can we fail, in the whole light of Scripture, to see what the difference is? "*My* Father, as by eternal Generation, ἄχρονος γέννησις; *your* Father, by adopting and regenerating grace in Me : *My* God, as by Paternal Deity, by relations within the Godhead, and also in the bright mystery of Incarnation ; *your* God, as in covenant through Me ; Mine, and so therefore yours, yours because Mine."

We are led to touch, with reverence, on a truth implied in this passage, though not directly taught in it, the Filial aspect of the Godhead of Christ. I humbly conceive that the words, "My Father and My God," have as much to do with the Divine as with the Human nature of the Son. Christ is God; yes, in all the fulness of the word. He is Eternal, Necessary, Uncreated, Absolute in every sacred attribute; Co-equal with the Father in "majesty, power and eternity," Blessed for ever. Yet He is THE SON. He is, while God, Filial. Unbeginning, He is yet eternally *of* the Father, and His blessed Being is in just such a sense subordinate that He is—with the "is" of eternity—the Son. Thought is lost, or rather silenced, when we come really in face of the revealed glory of the Godhead. But when we have just spelt out the revelation of It as it stands, we see in that revelation two truths most bright of all for us—the Godhead and the Sonship of the Lord our Saviour. And in the light of that view it is surely safe and Scriptural to see, in a passage like this, words which befit the voice of Jesus Christ speaking, not as Son of Man only, but as God the Son.

But if the doctrinal value of these words is thus large and precious, how great is their practical power and sweetness in personal application to the Christian's soul! Do we really take in, to some degree, what it is to know God the Father as the God and Father of our Lord Jesus Christ, and *in this respect* our God and Father too? To know the Father in beholding (θεωροῦντες) the Son? To love the Father in loving the Son? To rest on the Father in resting on the Son, on God the Son, on "the only begotten Son who is in the bosom of the Father"?

A very different view of God is this from that of *the mere* Theist. "The Absolute God," says Martin Luther,[1] "all men, who do not wish to perish, should fly from, because human nature and God Absolute are irreconcilable enemies (*infestissimi inimici*). From the Name of God we dare not shut out Christ. Not naked Deity but God robed and revealed in His word and promises we must lay hold upon, or inevitable despair must crush us. This God we can embrace, and behold, with joy and confidence; but Absolute Deity is as a wall of brass, on which we cannot strike without ruin."

How precious is that ancient, that old-fashioned faith, too often slighted under the unpopular designation "*orthodox*"—how precious, to the heart which craves, and discovers, a Saviour! In it the Lord is seen as not only God and Man, but *God the Son* and Man. He

[1] On Ps. li. 1; quoted by Professor Stanley Leathes, *Witness of the Old Testament to Christ*, p. 244. Dr Leathes remarks that Luther's "invaluable works were never more worthy of study than at the present crisis of the Church."

is revealed, He is believed in, as God the Son; not that we may worship Him less truly than we worship the Father, or trust Him less, or love Him less, but that we may all the more truly worship, trust, and love Him and His Father, who are One. He is the Eternal Son: who shall measure the love of Paternal Godhead for Filial? And—the Father "spared not His own (ἴδιον) Son, but delivered Him up for us all" (Rom. viii. 32); "so loving the world that He gave His only begotten Son." In the rapturous Te Deum we address our Redeemer as the Everlasting Son of the Father; and in that title we adore at once the love of the Giver and the love of the Given; and we feel that a Subordination, not of essence, but of relation, a Relationship just so far subordinate that it is filial, only intensifies our adoration of the Godhead of our Saviour. It shows us, through the fact of His Filial Godhead, something of the ocean of love within the Eternal Nature of the Triune; love in the divine Relationships within It; love in the outgoings towards us of such a salvation from It.

Is this too much of a digression? I know not how to avoid it, for the very attraction of the blessed theme. The meditation of Him, the Lord Christ the Son, is sweet; joy in the

Lord is kindled at it.[1] In gazing on Him as the Son we understand *a little*, as in a glimpse, of what the Father meant when, from the heavens He called Him "My Beloved." And if by divine mercy we have been drawn to love the Beloved of the Father, shall we not be glad? Shall we not take home for ourselves the joy of this message which He sent on the Easter morning to the bewildered beings whom yet He was not ashamed to call His brethren—" I ascend unto My Father and your Father, and unto My God and your God"? It is the voice of the Beloved.

With such an errand, then, does Mary leave the garden.

> She first, all-happy Magdalena, bore
> From Joseph's grot the bliss unheard before,
> And still her tidings was the broken tomb;
> And still, though ages roll,
> That message from the soul,
> And that alone, must chase the enfolding gloom.
> Jesus, our Lord, the First and Last,
> Thy rising work is past;
> Then present is our strength and rest,
> And all our future blest.

She comes, reporting to the disciples that she has seen the Lord, and that He said these things to her.

She obeyed at once. Quietly, with the joy of

---

[1] See Psalm civ. 34.

love (we seem to see her), she gives up her literal contact with His presence, and goes from the company of the risen Jesus Christ to the very different company of His mistaken and troubled disciples, all of whom, save Peter and John (and they, perhaps, were still apart), still lay in the cloud of their awful disappointment, and were not greatly disposed to see light through it. St Luke (xxiv. 11) tells us of the report of the women (and probably Mary's special message-bearing is included in that brief summary) as seeming to the disciples λῆρος, "nonsense"; and of course they said so to the messengers. Perhaps the first theory of James, and Philip, and Andrew was what long after was the theory of Renan, that the report was the product of illusion, and the illusion the product of feminine emotion. However, Mary went, in that spirit of meek but mighty confidence which is given to the soul now, as well as then, by the certainty in itself of the life and the love of Jesus. "He that believeth shall not make haste" (Isa. xxviii. 16); "we which have believed do enter into rest" (Heb. iv. 3), a rest full of power. All through that forenoon, probably, she saw her Lord no more; nor through that afternoon, which He spent upon the Emmaus road. And perhaps from time to time that day she heard much to distress her in the refusal of

"His brethren," many of them at least, to believe Him risen. Yet we are quite sure that it was a day of unimaginable joy for Mary Magdalene. Her own load of hopeless grief was gone. If He had dismissed her from His side, if He remained hour by hour out of sight, what did it matter, beside the gladness of knowing that He was risen, and alive for evermore? An hour, a few hours, ago she had loved Him with a love full of despair; now, with a love full of immortality. Then it was comparatively a blind affection, now she had a sunrise view of what He really was, and of what He had done, and would for ever do, for her. Then the past seemed all failure, the present solitude and ruin, the future a cruel gloom. Now past, present, and future were all filled with the work, the love, the triumph of her dear risen Lord. Then she could go to the others only to mingle her fears and tears with theirs, now she went as her Saviour's own commanded messenger to them, to constrain them to believe and be glad because of Him, and she bore witness to Him by her own joy. Her own burthen was now gone; how much better now she could bear theirs! Her own perplexities were passed away now for ever; how gently and tenderly, while with confidence, she could now wait for the time when He should be pleased (as, of course, He would be pleased) either to open their hearts to her message, or in some other way to reveal Himself to them!

I do not apologize for thus dwelling on some of the possibilities of that day, as spent by the first messenger of the Resurrection.[1] Our own hearts, surely, see in them more than possibilities, and they carry lessons of living power to ourselves as believers, not in ourselves, but in a risen Redeemer.

Throughout that day of joy and trial there must have been, for Mary, a wonderful conquest of joy over trial. She would be " at leisure from herself," and very full of Jesus Christ. She would be specially softened and sanctified, cut off delightfully from sinning in word or spirit, by the unselfish, adoring sense of His triumph, simply *as His*. It was not only that *she* was personally relieved, rescued, I might almost say immortalized already, by what she knew for herself; she knew now also something of the glory, the victory, the joy into which HE had entered who had once expelled seven devils from her. And this would more than fill the blank which *nature* might feel when His visible presence was left behind her in the garden. He, she knew, was safe in His own blood-bought

---

[1] See below, Appendix i.

victory, and was on His way to His own Father's throne. He had suffered; it had pleased the Lord, the Father, to bruise Him (Isa. liii. 10); He had died, going through all that death is, and more than death can ever be now to His followers; He had had to bear it all; His Agony and Death were now irrevocable facts. But so now also was His triumph. "The joy set before Him" had come. He was in the infinite repose of conquest over sin and death; He would need to die no more. And soon He would be receiving the eternal tribute of the praises of heaven, for He was going to the Father.

If all men disbelieved, yet was it all true *for Him*. And, though they disbelieved, they too would soon be worshipping with joy like hers; for He who had sent that message would not linger long behind it.

Nor did He do so. The Evangelist who has dismissed Peter and John now in turn dismisses Mary, never to name her again, for she has done her work for us. He brings us face to face once more with the Lord.

The day has drawn to its evening. Many have been its alarms and surprises, and half hopes, and troubled rumours, and obstinate reasonings of unbelief. And, now, as the shadows fall, the group of the Apostles, ten of the Twelve, and others (Luke xxiv. 33) with them, are together. There they are, gathered after scattering, and with some glad awakenings of faith and hope in their souls, for by that time the rumours of the Resurrection had begun to tell, and Peter and John were now with them (see Luke xxiv. 34).

They were assembled, perhaps in John's lodgings, perhaps in the chamber of the Last Supper. The Evangelist takes no pains to tell us, nor does he give us a single extraneous detail; for instance, the manner of entrance of St Luke's two travellers from Emmaus, who came in a little while before Jesus appeared. St John gives the scene just so as best to show us the Risen Lord Himself. And we will close this chapter with the mere translation of the wonderful record.

Verse 19. *So when it was evening, on that day, the first day of the week, and when the doors of the place where they were gathered had been shut because of their dread of the Jews, Jesus came and took His stand in* (ἔστη εἰς) *their midst, and says to them, Peace be to you. And as He said so He showed them His hands and His side. So the disciples rejoiced* (ἐχάρησαν), *seeing the Lord. So Jesus said to them again, Peace be to you. Even as the Father has sent Me out, I too send you. And as He said so He breathed a breath towards them, and says to them, Take (the) Holy Spirit. If you remit the sins of any, they are remitted to them; if you retain the sins of any, they are retained.*

Of course all study of details must be deferred. But let us at once carry away the fact of that scene and its blessing. In the hush of the deep evening, in that broad dimly-lighted chamber, where the anxious group are listening for the tread of the enemy, heavy or stealthy, upon the stairs, and preparing perhaps for such defence as Galilean courage even then might try, on a sudden the Holy One Himself is there. And we are there to see Him, and to be glad with them in Him. It is our privilege, our right, our possession. For us He has died and risen; He is about to ascend for us; He brings for us the gift of the Spirit.

To us He shows His hands and His side, and we read there our salvation, as truly as Peter, and John, and James, and all the once fugitive disciples, read theirs there that evening. Like them, we receive it wholly from Him. Like them, we behold the Lamb of God, sacrificed, risen, ascending to the heavens, and in that view we, like them, looking on Him whom *we* have pierced (Zech. xii. 10), step off from the unrest, the languor, the cowardice, of Christless self into the rest and joy of Jesus Christ.

One of the witnesses of that evening, many years later, wrote as follows (1 Pet. i. 3) to all the sharers of his faith: "Blessed be the God and Father of our Lord Jesus Christ, who, according to His abundant mercy, hath begotten us again to a living hope by the resurrection of Jesus Christ from the dead."

> Why walk in darkness? Has the dear light vanish'd
>   That gave us joy to-day?
> Has the great Sun departed? Has sin banish'd
>   His life-begetting ray?
>
> Lord, Thou art risen; but Thou descendest never;
>   To-day shines as the past;
> All that Thou wast Thou art, and shalt be ever,
>   Brightness from first to last.
>   *Bonar.*

VI

THE LORD IN THE CHAMBER.

IN our last study we only touched the narrative of the Saviour's appearance to the gathered company on the Resurrection evening. We now return to that narrative to consider it more in detail. And may He of whom we think approach us and speak to us through our meditation. In the evening shadows may He bring us His light. Even so come, Lord Jesus Christ. In the nightfall of change, of grief, of the sense of sin, and in spite of the doors which our ignorance or unbelief would shut, unwittingly, against Thee, come and speak to us that peace which the world, even at its best and purest, cannot give. Show us Thyself, and breathe into us Thy Spirit.

Verse 19. οὔσης οὖν ὀψίας: *So when it was evening.* The exact hour must be left uncertain, but probably it was an hour, or perhaps two hours, after sunset. The word ὀψία does not necessarily denote late evening. Indeed, in Mark i. 32 (ὀψίας, ὅτε ἔδυ ὁ ἥλιος), it is explicitly connected with the sunset. So again in Matt. xvi. 2, ὀψίας γενομένης λέγετε, Εὐδία, πυρράζει γὰρ ὁ οὐρανός : there the ruddy splendour of the sunset sky, with its afterglow, the sign of "a glorious morrow," is connected with the ὀψία. But on the other hand, to fix within *some* limits the time reference here, we must remember that St Luke supplies us with a note in his narrative of Emmaus. There the two disciples plead with their Stranger Friend to "abide with them," because it was "towards evening (πρὸς ἑσπέραν), and the day had declined" (xxiv. 29); and then followed the meal, and the revelation of Jesus, and their hurried return to Jerusalem, which could scarcely have taken less than an hour and a half in any case. Then came the Lord's appearance in the midst of the company at Jerusalem, an appearance certainly identical with that now before us. If Emmaus had been reached at sunset, or say an hour before it, the arrival in the chamber first of Cleopas and his friend and then of the Risen One may be placed at a time ranging from one to two hours after the sun had gone.

This, in Palestine, with its short twilight, would mean of course that it was now quite dark—very dark indeed, no doubt, in the byways of Jerusalem, and in the courtyards, and on the stairs of the houses. Through those deep shadows of the vernal night, if not already in the late afternoon, the Galilean disciples had found their way from their Passover lodgings here and there to the central meeting-place. Not the Apostles only had entered; there were "those that were with them" (Luke xxiv. 34). Perhaps it was a company of twenty or thirty. The holy women, probably, were of the number, just as we find them in Acts i. 14; the two from Emmaus made part of the group at the last moment; and there had entered also, very likely, several more of the inner circle of adherents. Not that a really large number, however, would be there on that first day of mingled hopes and fears. Thomas, we know, was absent, and many another less conspicuous disciple would naturally have felt and acted like him, in helpless grief, not to speak of positive fear for limbs and life.

We are not to think of the company as silent, in solemn expectation of the coming joy. The room, we gather from St Luke again (xxiv. 33—35), was a scene of conversation, of exclamation, of excitement. During the day now over Jesus had been appearing at intervals to one and another of His followers; Mary, the other women, Peter (Luke xxiv. 34), Cleopas, all had seen Him. Each might fail at first to convince all the rest, but the concurrence of witness would of course, above all when Peter joined it, begin to tell. So it had done, even by the time that Cleopas and his friend reached the city.

What a conversation it must have been, as all thronged together to hear more from each! And all the while they would be also listening, lest the gate of the court and the door of the room should be thrust open, and Roman guards or temple officials—"the captain of the Temple" and his men—should break in upon them.

So they mingled their joys and their fears in the large dimly-lighted room. (Lighted it was, in some measure, or they could not afterwards have *looked* so intently on their Master's scars; but no more light than was needful would be used in that anxious hour.)

But now there came a sudden hush. For while they were in full conversation (St Luke tells us this) then, says St John, JESUS came and ἔστη εἰς τὸ μέσον—stepped into the midst, and there took His stand. Such is the brief account; we shall gain little by striving to realize every detail. What would we not give to see, as if in living presence, through the glass of a pictorial narrative, the RISEN ONE as He was? To gaze on the very body of His Resurrection, the "flesh and bones" which He literally had, and in which the scars were visible and palpable? To see the sameness and yet difference in the frame and form of the Great Shepherd brought again from the dead? But we cannot, we must not. The wonderful narrative strikes us alternately by its details and by its silence. Notes of time, place, and individual character are given in abundance, but gratifications of mere curiosity, especially about the aspect of our Redeemer, are with equal care withheld. It is as it ever is with Scripture; the nature, the glory of Jesus Christ we have given us, for this we need. We do not really need a photograph of His form, and it is not given. Enough to know that the sacred Body was real, was human, was identical—that it had been slain, but now was alive for evermore.

So we are constrained to look, not upon a picture, but upon the fact—JESUS there, in the midst of them.

How had He entered? St John does not tell us. Possibly the simple reason of his silence is that he did not know. He knew that the doors (of courtyard and of room) had been fastened, and yet that Jesus now stood in the room. But whether with mysterious speed and silence He had opened those doors, or whether without opening them He had willed that the material of His risen Body should pass through their material, probably the Evangelist could not tell. Only it is plain that he intends us to think that there was *some* mystery in the matter.

We may incline to either of the two alternatives. The secret opening of the doors may seem the more in harmony of the two with the perfect simplicity otherwise of the narrative of the Resurrection visits. It would be mysterious and indeed miraculous; for the doors were well fastened, manifestly, from within. But it would be, so to speak, the more conceivable, the more simple, act of power.

On the other hand, the possibility of the second alternative must not for a moment be denied as if it were (what no Scripture miracle will ever be found to be) a contradiction to the laws of thought. One plea for it is that it seems as certain as anything can be, without a distinct assertion, that the Risen Lord left the sepulchre *before the stone was moved.* Was *this* a contradiction to the laws of thought? It would be so were we called on to believe that the stone and the Body quite precisely filled the same space at the same moment; the particles of the one coinciding with those of the other. But is there not open to us a different theory, to be held with reverent modesty? Grant to the risen Body a mysterious subtlety of material (and remember that even the least subtle body is not really solid, not really without interstices between particle and particle), and we can surely see the line of abstract possibility in which the supposed miracle would run.

I make these somewhat obvious remarks just because it seems to me that *no other* miracle, recorded or predicted, even tempts us to doubt it on *this* ground, the ground of apparent abstract or mental impossibility. The raising of the dead presents no such difficulty when the Lord of life is the Agent, directly or indirectly. But the conception of two bodies occupying really, atom for atom, the same space, *is* a contradiction to the laws under which the Creator has bid us think and know. And so it is worth while to notice that at least one known fact, the fact that no material body is in the strictest sense solid, shows us that such a conception is not demanded by the view that the doors that night were not opened.

We may linger a moment or two longer over this question, because the passage (on the latter hypothesis) has been made use of very naturally in the search of arguments for the subtle tenet of transubstantiation. It has been almost assumed that if we can believe that the Lord's Resurrection body passed through a "solid" door, we can believe *anything* about it; we can believe it to have nothing to do with laws of space; we can believe it to be everywhere, or practically everywhere, and to be present in, with, under anything.

But, in the first place, such reasoning begins, surely, with a neglect of "*the proportion* of the faith." For one proof which Scripture gives us of mysterious qualities in the Lord's blessed Body of the Resurrection, it gives many proofs of, so to speak, simple qualities in it. And not one incident—not *this* incident, most certainly —can be adduced to show that it was ever in two places at the same time. Bodily, He was in Emmaus and Jerusalem, not at once, but successively, so far as anything goes that we know. "He *came*," and that one expression, used so often and so familiarly, denies the ubiquity of His Body. Subtlety of particles and organization, mysterious speed, mysterious invisibility, these are wonderful things, but not at all (in a strict sense of the word) inconceivable. The presence of a human body in more than two places at once is strictly inconceivable. And is it not the case, as I said above, that *never*, unless in this case alone, does Scripture miracle imply what is strictly inconceivable? If so, is not the ubiquitarian theory, or anything like it, out of proportion with the faith?

Is not that "faith," taken as a whole, in this matter of Christ's Presence, as simple as it is divine? The Lord our Saviour is indeed ubiquitous as God, as God the Son. And His Divine Nature is united to His Human Nature. So He is everywhere present as God, being also Man. But the Lord our Saviour is *corporeally absent*, in the main aspects of Scripture doctrine; as to His blessed Body (His "natural" Body, as the last rubric of the Communion Office calls it; that is, His non-mystical Body, His mystical Body being the Church), He is markedly withdrawn from us for a season; with the promise of a glorious return of that Body to the range and ken of our senses, when He shall "*come.*"

With deep and tender reverence toward God, and sympathy towards man, let every discussion about the nature and work of the Sacrament of the Holy Table be carried on. There is nothing more perfectly irreligious than bitterness in religion; assuredly there is nothing which more effectually shuts out from the heart the joyful presence of Him who vouchsafes (Eph. iii. 17) to dwell in it by faith. But to avoid a bitter eagerness does not mean either to be indifferent to objective truth, or to go on the principle that a vague uncertainty is ever *in itself* a spiritual gain. If, for instance, it is the fact, as I think it is, that the New Testament indicates that "the Body" of the blessed Communion is not the Body as now glorified, but the Body as once crucified,[1] it cannot be a gain to us to think quite indistinctly about it, or not to be of one mind with Scripture about it. And surely it is happily possible to combine distinctness of Scriptural conviction with that gentleness and sympathy which the Scriptures, and which the ordinance of the Holy Supper, so pressingly and delightfully enjoin on the Christian, and which the Christian who "abides in Christ" *shall* find supplied out of the fulness of His Lord.

But now let us come back from this excursion. Let us fix our glad and worshipping eyes on the Risen One standing there in that room in the midst of His followers. However He had come, HE WAS THERE; that was the point. Let us

[1] See at large the late Dr Vogan's learned book, *The True Doctrine of the Eucharist.*

thank God if we can humbly say the same of our hearts: However my Lord came in, He is here now, dwelling in my heart by faith, manifesting to me His death for me, saying to me, It is I; thy sins be forgiven thee; receive the Spirit. However He came, whether He passed through the door, or softly opened it, or broke it down; whether my conversion to Him was a lightning-like burst of day in night, or a calm sunrise hour, or a slow clearing of a misty sky into the blue; one thing I know, the Sun shines now; JESUS is here. He has come into the midst, and I am glad, for I see the Lord.

He took His stand in their midst. What a place was this for the Risen Lord to take! He, so holy, so triumphant, comes "into the midst" of that throng of unworthy sinners! It is indeed a wonderful sight, Jesus Christ come back "into the midst of them." Yet it is His chosen stand, willingly taken, with the willing joy of love. They have grieved Him, but, with a conquering Saviour's love, He loves them, and so their company is sweet to Him. And what He was, He is.

Sweet indeed is the sound of His first utterance to them: *He says to them, Peace be to you.* It is no mere salutation, but a divine reality. The Speaker is also the Reason. "He is their

Peace" (Eph. iii. 14). "The God of Peace has brought Him from the dead, through the blood of the everlasting covenant" (Heb. xiii. 20), shed three days before.

St Luke, our welcome supplement to St John in this whole scene, tells us how much they needed that word. Their *first* sight of Him was full of alarm; they thought that they were gazing on a disembodied spirit (xxiv. 37); so mysterious had been His coming, so sudden was His visible manifestation. And to have seen "a spirit," however it might have resembled the living Jesus—yes, even to have seen *His* bodiless human "Spirit,"[1] would not have been, properly, to see THE LORD. It would not have meant any victory over death. It would not have been, in the least, a Resurrection.

So also (let us remember, as we pass on) with the soul now. He who can and does speak Peace must be a living not a visionary Saviour. He must be the Christ, not of fancy, not of aspiration even, but of both history and revelation; literally risen, living, coming. Not "a spirit," but the Lord.

And now, "this same Jesus," Reality not

[1] Observe this as a perfectly incidental witness to the *intelligence* of the disciples in their faith in the bodily Resurrection of their Lord.

Vision, speaks peace to these frightened and troubled hearts. What a peace it was! "Peace, peace," as the prophet says (Isa. xxvi. 3), a double peace; the peace of the finished Work and of the living Presence.

Absolute indeed was the *gift* of such peace. They had learnt effectually that He must and could give it, and only He. Nothing of their own could do so. The moment they lost (as they thought) HIM, what comfort had they from themselves? They had worked miracles, they had preached a sublime message, they had been centres of spiritual influence. But all these things, divorced from Him "in the midst of them," could only by the contrast intensify their gloom. The fire and energy of Peter, the intense affection of Magdalene — were these sources of peace, on the supposition that Jesus was gone? No; each fine characteristic of the disciple would become only the side which felt the loss most bitterly; which felt most deeply that there is "no peace" apart from Him.

But now He came to give peace; to speak it as His gift, and to prove its validity as such.

For (verse 20) τοῦτο εἰπών, *as He said so*, with the words, *He showed them His hands and His side*. The holy Body was robed, and so as to hide the hands and side. Now He drew back,

He lifted up, the raiment, and they saw the certificates of His agony. He showed the "glorious scars," partly no doubt *for identification*. As they gazed in the lamplight at those deep clefts (the narrative of Thomas's doubt and conversion shows they were still deep *hollow* wounds), bloodless, we must suppose, and with none of the fever of wounds about them,[1] yet still wounds indeed; as they examined with their eyes (and fingers? Luke xxiv. 39) the rent side, and saw, as it were, the light through the sacred hands, they knew Him in truth for "this same Jesus." And that by itself was sweet indeed, even as it is now when the disciple's soul realizes that, after all these ages, it is dealing still with the same Person identically who died for us and rose again.

But also, surely, He showed them His wounds for a further purpose; to bear in upon them the thought of *the way in which* He had brought them that peace which now was theirs. There He stood before them, their living Lord, immortally living. But He was also now what before He had not been, their living Lord who had for them been slain. Such was to be "His name for ever, His memorial to all generations"

[1] The Risen Body is nowhere described as "flesh *and blood*."

now. What a paradox! Never through the eternal ages will the Lord of Life be parted from the remembrance of His Death, and from the praises of His people because He died. And never let Him and His Death be parted in our thought and love now. While we realize with joy that He lives, that He is beside us and within us, let Him be ever to us still "the Lamb that was slain," "the Shepherd brought from the dead," the Lord who, "that He might indeed be Lord," be Master, "*died* and revived" (Rom. xiv. 9). When we use Him, in His indwelling power, as our life, and as our one way of victory over sin, still let Him be to us the Lord who "loved me, and *gave Himself* for me" (Gal. ii. 20).

He shewed them His hands and His side. So *the disciples rejoiced* (ἐχάρησαν, aorist, a definite *act* of joy), *seeing the Lord.* THE LORD; that name by which more than ever now they loved to call Him.

The two great blessings flowed together, in His presence; Εἰρήνη, Χαρά, Peace, Joy. Showing His wounds, He spoke the peace. Seeing Him, they knew the joy.

Verse 21. Jesus now speaks again. The outbreak of untold joy was, as to its expression, over; what a scene of tears, and wonder, and shame, and recognition, and worshipping praise it must have been! But now He speaks again, and the word again, calm and articulate, is *Peace be to you*. Their very joy, in its deep agitation, needed this—a clear, definite assurance of the strong *basis* of such gladness, a certainty that it was caused from without, *His* gift, the issue of *His* work.

Speaking peace, He gives them at once, bound up with it in love, Duty. *Even as the Father has sent Me out, I too send you.* Even so. As I was to be His Representative in My work on earth, so you are now to be Mine. As I was His Ambassador in "the days of My flesh," you are to take My place. Ὑπὲρ Χριστοῦ πρεσβεύετε, "be ambassadors in Christ's stead" (2 Cor. v. 20). And be so in Christ's spirit. Your duty, your obedience, is to be your sphere of joy, as His was.

That duty, let us observe, was not given them till they had seen in Him their joy. "They rejoiced, seeing the Lord"; "Now send I you."

Such was our Lord Jesus Christ's commission to His true flock, His true Church. Assuredly it was not to the Apostles only, however specially; it was to all that "blessed company of believing people." "Even so send I you." Every believer is to be a messenger under that commission, and to take the Risen Lord as his message.

Then, with an act of divinely simple symbolism, He "conveys" to them (makes over to them, as by an act and deed of gift, a physical visible action at once to instruct and strengthen their faith) the Holy Spirit. Their embassy, their message-bearing, their representation of Him, was to be done only and truly "in the Spirit," if it was to be rightly done at all.

He breathed a breath towards them, and says to them, Take the Holy Spirit.

Are we to understand that this action of the Lord's, with His spoken word, did literally then and there infuse the Spirit's power into them? I dare not say not. But do not the circumstances rather favour the view that the incident was divinely symbolical, and was rather a prophecy of Pentecost than a part-gift before Pentecost? His *mission* of His people into the world was, in a sense, not to take actual effect till Pentecost. Was not the same the case with this quasi-sacramental "gift" of the Spirit to His people? Was it not a guarantee rather than a then-and-there infusion? If so, the case is instructive in the study of sacramental truth.

But now, how does He proceed? Verse 23

If you remit the sins of any, they are remitted to them; if you retain the sins of any, they are retained.

On these deep words I only lightly touch In a few brief paragraphs, calling attention to some leading considerations about them.

(i.) They are a commission to the Church, to the Church as the Representative and Witness on earth of the Risen Lord Jesus; not to Apostles only, but to all true believers. We have already seen this, as we have recalled St Luke's evidence to the fact that other disciples were present with the Apostles.

(ii.) There must therefore be a sense, and that a very important and conspicuous sense, in which every true disciple is called upon to act on the Easter commission. Whatever remitting and retaining means, it has something to do, as God shall show the way, with every Christian's life and work.

(iii.) This consideration interferes not at all with the conception of an ordered, ordering, specially-commissioned Christian pastorate. The pastoral office is as old as Christianity. The same Risen Lord who, when He ascended on high, "gave some as apostles," also "gave some as pastor-teachers, to equip the saints for (their) work of service, for the upbuilding of

Christ's Body" (Eph. iv. 11, 12). And the Christian pastorate, despite all the defects and sins of Christian pastors, has assuredly proved itself, in fact, to be a mighty and salutary factor in the Church. To put only one most simple side of the matter forward; the fact that a host of Christian men year after year are solemnly, by chosen representatives of the Church, separated and dedicated for their whole lives to special thought, special labour, special guiding function, special speech for Christ, has certainly had an effect beyond calculation in the coherence and force of the work of the Christian Church.

But to say that it is the special office of a class or order to proclaim the message of our Master is not to say that that message is not to be proclaimed by all who belong to Him.

(iv.) This declaration, this commissioned declaration, of His message, with its alternative of condemnation or pardon, death or life, is, I am convinced, the work here entrusted by Him to His Church.

That it does not mean, certainly at its heart and centre, a private judicial sacerdotal absolution or its reverse, I am sure. First, because the Scriptures, fairly interrogated, give no clear evidence that such a function was claimed or exercised by the Apostles, or enjoined by them on even the earliest presiding pastors. Secondly, because such a delegation to man of the judicial power of God, if it is not to be a mere name, a something worse than useless, would necessarily involve the need that the absolver and retainer should be, as such, inspired—gifted with a special discernment both of the nature of the sin of the soul and of the sincerity of the soul, and not of its sincerity only, but of its self-knowledge, its truth or its error in estimating and describing its sin.

I do not think that either Scripture or experience at all assures us that Christian pastors, as such, are by any means thus inspired; that they have, as such, any supernatural intuition into the self-knowledge of the human soul.

But if it be the duty of every Christian, in his or her path of intercourse and influence, to "retain sins" and "remit sins" in the sense of pointing out, as a living witness, the Scripture terms of pardon and peace to a sorely needing world—here is indeed an intelligible as well as a most blessed commission; and it is a work as to which the Acts and Epistles are full of suggestions, while they are silent about a sacerdotal function of confession and absolution.

Of the special and adapted bearing of the

words as used in the ordination of the Anglican presbyter, and again in the formula which he is directed to utter, under very peculiar and guarded conditions, in the Visitation of the Sick, I scarcely speak at all here. But it may not be out of place to point out how clear the witness of Church History is to the fact that in such a connexion the drift of the word is towards "remission" and "retention" *from the point of view of the Christian Society;* towards guarding the central hearth, so to speak, even the Table of the Lord, from unworthy intrusion. And even thus, it may be remembered, the formula was not introduced into the Ordinal for the Presbyter till the thirteenth century.[1]

But this is a digression indeed. I recur to that view of the Lord's commission, which, alike for the pastor and the layman, is at once the simplest and the most sacred—the carrying to the world, as by a messenger who is also a living witness, of the message of the grace of God. Specially for my ministerial brethren I venture thus to point to it once more. May our idea of our ministry never be lowered from this; never

[1] See a learned sermon by the Bishop (Reichel) of Meath, *The History and Claims of the Confessional*, 1884.

allowed to sink into the idea of a merely administrative and ceremonial function, or into that of only philanthropic enterprise. May we live and labour as those who deal indeed with sin and with salvation, and in our Master's Name; as those who know in our own instance how the human heart needs remission, and how it must and does find it in Christ alone. May we minister as those who know their own souls and their own Saviour, so as to enable them to deal with the souls of others; above all, who can say, as those first disciples of the Chamber could, "We have seen the Lord, who was dead but is alive for evermore, and our heart is glad in the sight of Him; now then (2 Cor. v. 20, 21) we are ambassadors in His stead; in His stead we pray you, be reconciled to God. For God hath made Him to be sin on our behalf who knew no sin, that we might be made the righteousness of God in Him."

VII

THE EASTER MESSAGE—THOMAS.

I DO not propose to retrace the lines of comment on verses 22, 23, offered in the last chapter. Let me only add to them the remark that if the conclusions then suggested are substantially true, we are led to the thought that the commission given to the Church is given to it, practically, as it is (Article XX.) *testis et conservatrix divinorum librorum,* "a" (the Article in its English does not say "the") "witness and keeper of Holy Writ." Such a witness and safe-keeper the Church is, undoubtedly; a character too often either forgotten or greatly mistaken. Some Christians think of Scripture as bound up with the Church visible more than it is, some as bound up with it less than it is. Some extend the meaning of Article XX. so far as to make the witness and safe-keeper to be, *therefore and as such*, the only qualified *interpreter;* a gratuitous inference, as if a librarian as such were an adequate expositor. Some, on the other hand (it may be from a deep and joyful experience of the living power of the written Word), forget too much its intimate connexion and, so to speak, cohesion with the living, breathing Congregation of Christian disciples. No doubt it can happen, and in detached cases it does happen, that the Book acts altogether apart from the immediate action of the Church. I know, from first-hand report, of instances in which a Bible has been the solitary means through which Christianity, orthodox and living, has been learnt by one who was an untaught heathen when the Book almost literally fell into his hands. But even in such an instance we trace an indirect co-operation of the Christian Church; for without its existence it is most unlikely that Scripture, as we have it, would have been largely copied, preserved amidst the storms of history, and widely dispersed. On the human side, every copy of the Bible is connected with the existence of the Church, as a condition to its existence. And then, in the immense preponderance of actual experiences, the written Word is brought home to the individual by the spoken witness of the Church, coming (as of course it must ordinarily come) through the voice of some other individual, who in his turn has already been similarly approached. Practically, it is the Christian parent, or friend, or teacher, or expositor, who, in the vastly larger number of cases, is to the individual the "witness" as well as "keeper" of Holy Writ, saying, "This is the Word of God; I have received it; I pass it on to you." It is an individual who speaks, or writes, but an individual who, knowingly or not, has been helped to his or her own realization of the written treasure by the conditions and aids of Christian membership, and who is thus in some sense, in turn, an organ of that membership in its work of witnessing and keeping.

Doubtless, if every living witness and every Christian uninspired book were to vanish from the earth to-morrow, the Book would still prove its own undying and independent power. But would it, in the actual workings of human life, speak to man nearly as often, or as widely, as before?

It is one thing to dream (it *is* a dream) of a Church-interpretation of Scripture such that the reverent and prayerful soul *cannot* get at the true sense of Scripture without it.

It is another thing when what we assert is a connexion of Scripture with the visible Congregation of Christ, such that the world's acquaintance with the Word, reverence for it, and benefit by it, is indefinitely increased and assured by that connexion.[1]

It is then this character of the disciples of Christ, and of their Community, as the actual witnesses and guardians of the revelation of Christ, which is referred to specially, if I am right, in the passage before us. The revelation of Christ is above all things a revelation with a view to the remission or retention of sin. It reveals, with infallible certainty, the way of remission, the means to it, and, by consequence, how to miss it. The terms of the revelation are sure; its absolution or condemnation is divine. When St Paul, for example, or St John so instructs me as to assure me, penitent and believing, that my sins are forgiven, I am to be as sure of it as if Christ stood by me and spoke the words. And when a Christian pastor, in his ministry, and when also a Christian friend, in

---

[1] It may not be out of place to refer to Augustine's well-known words, *Ego Evangelio non crederem nisi me Catholicæ Ecclesiæ commoveret auctoritas*. (*Contra Epistolam Manichæi quæ Fundamenti dicitur*, cap. v.) The ample teaching of Augustine on Scripture assures us that he by no means intended by this that the Church is above Scripture, or that Scripture owes its divine authority to the Church. But he felt it an all-important credential to Scripture that it came to him as a fact through the historic Christian Society as that Society's rule of faith.

conversation or by example, *brings home* to my thought and heart such an apostolic—*i.e.* such a divine—absolution, or, again, some corresponding apostolic condemnation of my state or of an act in my state, he is doing me not an accidental service, but one divinely instituted, and implied in the fact that our Lord willed that His followers should be a Community, and should live and work with His Word in their possession.

Two reflections may be offered before the subject is quitted.

First, this *diffusion* of the witnessing and keeping office over the whole Christian congregation is no contradiction to the divine institution of an ordained and thus far separated Ministry—a Ministry which has a function full of life and blessing, concentrating the witness of the Congregation, and securing in a degree otherwise impossible, or at best most precarious, the order and the continuity of Christian worship. Hence, as we have already remembered, the commission to the Church is, in our Ordinal, not unlawfully given with special emphasis to the Christian presbyter; though this was not done in any known ordination ritual for presbyters before the thirteenth century.

Secondly, on the other hand, whatever is true

of the remitting and retaining efficacy of the Church's true witness to Scripture, and true articulation of the message of Scripture, this must be at least as deeply true of the direct witness of Scripture to the soul as the man reads it and ponders it for himself. Of the Oracle itself we may truly say, "Whosoever sins it doth remit, they are remitted unto them." I quote some wise words of Doddridge's, written on this passage one hundred and fifty years ago, in that often useful commentary, his *Expositor:* "Let us try our state by the character laid down in the inspired writings; in which sense we may assure ourselves that if our sins are declared to be remitted, they are remitted. And if indeed they are so, we need not be much concerned by whom they are retained. . . . Men may claim a power which God never gave, and which these words are far from implying. But whatever the sentence they may pass, they whom God blesseth are blessed indeed."

This whole subject is one of continual, and in our time of acute and special, importance. A properly sacerdotal theory of the Christian Ministry, in all parts of such a theory, and not least in that of a judicial absolution supposed to convey divine forgiveness, puts a human intermediation between man and God where God would have man see the one Mediator only. It is a contradiction to the sacred first principles of the Gospel.

Meanwhile may our Lord in mercy shorten the days of controversy, and utterly abolish in us that which likes controversy for its own sake ; and may He lengthen, till they fill our lives, the sweet hours in which we for ourselves enjoy in glad consciousness, and so are able gladly to assert to others, the holy certainties of the remission of sins for the Name's sake of the Only Begotten of the Father, who died for us and rose again.

But now let us pass at once to some view of a scene which will indeed carry us into the pure light of a direct view of the Lord Jesus Christ, seen in His living glory. We arrive at the record of the doubt and the belief of Thomas, verses 24—29.

Verse 24. *But Thomas, one of the Twelve, whose name means Twin, was not with them when Jesus came. So the other disciples began to say* (ἔλεγον) *to him, We have seen the Lord. But he said to them, Unless I see in His hands the print of the nails, and insert*[1]

---

[1] Βάλλειν appears never quite to lose a certain *force* of meaning. Here ἐὰν μὴ βάλω is not merely "unless I *put*," but almost " unless I *push.*"

my finger into the print of the nails, and insert my hand into His side, I will never believe (οὐ μὴ πιστεύσω). *And after eight days again the disciples were indoors, and Thomas with them. Jesus comes, while the doors were fastened, and took His stand in the midst, and said, Peace be unto you. Then He says to Thomas, Bring your finger hither, and see My hands; and bring your hand and insert it into My side; and do not become unbelieving, but believing. Thomas answered and said to Him, My Lord and My God. Jesus says to him, Because you have seen Me, Thomas, you have believed; happy such as saw not, and believed.* Ver. 30. *Now Jesus did many other signs besides in His disciples' presence, which have not been written in this book. But these have been written that you may believe that Jesus is the Christ, the Son of God, and that, believing, you may have life in His name.*

Of this passage I do not attempt any detailed exposition in this chapter; it will be more possible to do so in the next. At present I merely take up for notice some of its outstanding facts and lessons, asking the Risen Lord to grant writer and reader to realize His presence "in the midst," and to adore Him from the soul as our, nay as my, Lord and God.

We note, then, as often before, the concurrent brevity and minuteness of the record. Its brevity: no remarks or explanations are offered with reference to the absence of Thomas; just the fact is given, as necessary to explain the sequel. We are left to conjecture for ourselves why he was away. And conjecture surely says that his absence at such a time cannot have been mere accident. It was probably an expression of individual character, an act of that peculiar independence passing into self-will which we trace throughout his sketched portrait in this Gospel. I should not think that the mind of Thomas was one in which there was a strong tendency to doubt the miraculous, a Sadducean mind; but rather that he was a man decidedly apt to fall back upon himself, suspicious of over-influence from others, perhaps with something of that morbid honesty (if the phrase is permissible) which doubts because another believes, doubts because it fears, or seems to itself to fear, that it may accept reasons for belief which are good only for another. Such a character, I venture to take it, was expressed in that marked absence. Reports were about that Jesus had risen. Jesus he dearly, ardently loved (chap. xi. 16), whatever mistakes he made about Him. Perhaps the first notion of His Resurrection may

I

have struck bright and glad upon Thomas, as a notion. But with equal likelihood he may have decided against the reports for that very reason: "Too good to be true—so good that the wish must have fathered the assertion." So he would fortify himself with the reflection that his associates had done just this, had believed because they wished. Then he would unconsciously and easily pass from the spirit of grief to the spirit of pride, pride in his firmness and caution of thought, in his courageous willingness to be in the dark if dark it must be. Neither accident, nor intellectual scepticism, but grief passing into a sort of melancholy pride—such seems to me a probable account of the absence of Thomas.

All this, however, if true, is unrecorded by the pen of St John, in his tranquil brevity. Yet on the other hand, what minute traits of individuality we have in these few touches! How truly Thomas stands out as a real character, altogether different from Peter, for example, and from John; not for a moment to be taken for a mere reflection or echo of another personage. This is not only proof of veracity, of the firm reality which lies as a rock beneath the beautiful narrative. It is not only evidence that we have a record of facts before us, indicated in these brief touches not of art, but nature—for such nature-copying art *was not*, most surely, in Christian circles (if anywhere) when this Book was written. It is a phenomenon not only of fact, but of instruction and consolation. The individualities of the Apostles Peter, John, Thomas, Nathanael, Paul, are representative. And the fact that they were, each and all, subdued to the same adoring love of Jesus Christ is a representative fact. Were the Apostles for us so many mere names, so many lay-figures attired in Galilean costume and grouped around the Lord, their recorded faith would *teach* us very little. But they are " men of like feelings " with us, $\delta\mu οιοπαθεῖς\ ἡμῖν$ (James v. 17), like present-day people in their marked differences from one another. And the Lord Jesus found them all out, and they all found out Him; the one Lord, absolute and unalterable, and yet precisely the right Friend and Saviour for each of these persons.

Such a record as this may be used in the divine hand to remedy two very possible mistakes.

(i.) We are apt sometimes, in thinking, praying, speaking for the benefit of the souls of others, to forget too much the differences of character; to expect and to demand that characters the most diverse from our own shall not only reach the same results, but shall reach them by the same steps, in the same order. A man who has suffered much from intellectual clouds and conflicts, sometimes perhaps to be traced to indolence and half-heartedness, is often tempted to insist, as it were, that some friend now seeking after Christ shall feel just the same difficulties before he attains the light. Strange to say, such an attitude is possible, instead of that of the prayer and longing that into the light we now enjoy, holy and happy, this soul may step by any path our Master shall choose, and the sooner the better, if it be His will.

A mind, again, which has had little or no experience of such trials (and this exemption is sometimes a sign of mental health and strength, not of blindness or immaturity) is apt not seldom to grow impatient and unsympathetic in contact with one of the opposite cast. Let it not be so. True, you are not obliged to experience the conflict with the legions of doubt. But you should thoughtfully watch that conflict, and pray, like Moses on the hill, while Joshua was battling in the valley. You should recognize with respect a different character, training, position; not to doubt whether such a heart needs the same

Christ and the same salvation, but to bear with its different pace, its circuitous route, as it comes towards Him and to Him.

(ii.) On the other hand, are not Christian believers often tempted sorely in the other direction, tempted to too keen a suspicion, too serious an estimate of differences of character, in the presence of Christianity and Christ? Are we never disposed to say, practically, to ourselves—however whisperingly—that this man or that is so entirely different from myself that he never can, he never will, see Christ, His love, His redemption, as clearly and as gladly as I see it? And then perhaps the thought has already crept in, "and he never *need* do so."

This is fatalism under a veil. It makes a man's character his fate. It ignores the free and divine action of the Eternal Spirit upon men. It practically forgets the positive assurances of the Lord Jesus Christ that there is for every human soul a most urgent need that it should come to Him, and deal with Him.

This fatalism, a branch of a subtle and far-spread disease, we are helped to resist, to give the lie to, by this same wonderful record of the individualities of the Apostles. They, or at least the leaders of these leaders, were sharply and deeply differenced from each other.

And the Lord Jesus dealt with them in widely different ways. But He led them all to the same end—Himself; Himself seen and known by each as his all in all, his peace, his joy, his power, his purity, his Lord and God.

With admirable vividness this comes out in their artlessly-recorded words and deeds. How different was Thomas in mental and moral cast from John! Yet it is John who observes, who records with loving care, and so embraces, as it were, for his own the final faith of Thomas. How different was Thomas from Paul, the Galilean boatman from the marvellous youth of Cilicia trained into the Pharisaic expert in the school of Gamaliel; the rugged peasant-mind from him in whom the pride of the genius, the savant, and the zealot were, till grace changed him, all combined! And very different was their intercourse with Jesus, and with the followers of Jesus. But by "this same Jesus" they were both led into the same blessed results as regards faith in Him. "My Lord and my God," exclaims Thomas, at once adoring and appropriating, as true faith should ever do. "I live," writes Paul (Gal. i. 20), "by faith in the Son of God, who loved me, and gave Himself for me," adoring and also appropriating the same Person with the same heaven-given simplicity of faith; *his* pride also quite broken up, *his* difficulties also quite done away in the sunlight of Christ, *his* inmost heart also freely opened to learn what God would have him learn of the glory and the love of His Only Begotten.

For the present we close the Gospel again. But at least we have already gathered some fresh encouragement to patience and to faith from this first view of the story of St Thomas. May we be, for this our study, at once better able to sympathize with the differing characters and circumstances of others, and yet, all the while, more sure that, each and all, they need Christ, and the same Christ, with an absolute need. Above all, let us be sure of Him, trustful of Him, certain that He knows the way and holds the key, however impenetrable this or that mind or heart may seem to us. The more we recollect and realize these things, the better we shall, on the one hand, delight to do what we can to bear our humble witness to such a Redeemer, and the more truly, on the other hand, will our Christian witness be borne not to ourselves but to Christ Jesus our Lord.

Meanwhile, let us thank God, who commanded the light to shine out of darkness, that out of the darkness of the Apostle's doubts, and out of the darkness of the doubts of many a doubter since, He has brought forth light, the light of fresh and living evidences of the presence, the patience, the love, the glory of His dear Son. We may thankfully breathe as our own the prayer of the Church, written by the Reformers, and appointed for the memorial day of the once-perplexed disciple :

Almighty and everlasting God, who for the more confirmation of the faith didst suffer Thy holy Apostle Saint Thomas to be doubtful in Thy Son's Resurrection; Grant us so perfectly and without all doubt to believe in Thy Son Jesus Christ, that our faith in Thy sight may never be reproved. Hear us, O Lord, through the same Jesus Christ, to whom, with Thee and the Holy Ghost, be all honour and glory, now and for evermore. Amen.

VIII

THOMAS AND THE LORD.

We began in our last chapter to study the narrative of the doubt and the faith of Thomas, and remarked the strong individuality of the Apostle's character as it is indicated by St John. It is from St John only that we get any such information about the man; the other Evangelists and the Acts contain mere mentions of his name. In St John it occurs seven times, and in three cases it is given with the translation, Didymus, Twin. Is it possible that the Evangelist sees a moral significance in the name, as if it suggested a certain doubleness in the mind where love and mistrust were both at once so strong? Not that duplicity in any other sense is traceable in Thomas; his was anything but a character of guile.

In two other scenes in this Gospel, as we remember, Thomas appears, so to speak, in character. In xi. 16 he proposes to the others to accompany the Lord into Judea at a dangerous time: "Let us also go, that we may die with him;" a brief sentence, in which we see combined a resolution almost petulant, an intense devotion to his Lord's person, *and* great mistakes as to His nature and power. In xiv. 5 he seems to interrupt the Master in the midst of His words about the heavenly home and His purpose to "go and prepare" it for His followers: "Lord, we know not whither Thou goest, and how can we know the way?" Here again is the mind which shapes boldly to itself, and almost brusquely expresses, the difficulty or doubt which it feels. One other mention of Thomas in this Gospel must be recalled—xxi. 2. He is there the second name in that blessed company which met the Risen Jesus in the early morning by the lake-side. Is not this a beautiful and touching close to the notices of the Apostle? He has ceased to be the self-asserting, self-separating doubter. He is happy now to be just a brother with his brethren; and so he is privileged to enjoy, without delay, without reproof, that heavenly interview. Of this more hereafter.

We turn now to the narrative before us.

Verse 24. *But Thomas, one of the Twelve,*

whose name means Twin, was not with them when Jesus came.

"One of the *Twelve*": their, so to speak, official title, though, alas, they were now only eleven. This distinctive mention of the Twelve may suggest to us that, when just above and below the Evangelist speaks of "the disciples," he means the little company at large, and not only the Apostles.

I will not repeat what was said in our last chapter about the probable causes of Thomas' absence, only remarking again that in his mental frame we see, surely, the recent mental frame of all the disciples, but expressed more definitely and resolutely. He did but speak out, or rather act out, what had been deep in the hearts of all—a sense of tremendous disappointment, a deep and gloomy despondency, with the immediate impulse to separate rather than to combine.

Nothing can be more certain than that this impulse to separate would have had full sway finally, and very soon, if no magnificent antidote to the despair of Friday had come into the midst of them. The shame as well as pain of having embarked in a great mistake would have made them loth to meet and see each other's faces for long together. And the terrible act of Judas must have given them for a time a sense of mutual suspicion. If Judas had proved untrue, might not another, might not others? Those who had so often misconstrued the Master might easily suspect their fellow-servants.

In short, they were ready to disperse "every man to his own." They would have diverged, no doubt, in very different moods: some sullen, some tender, some quite silent, others seeking to explain everything. And had they done so, and had some rumours of that obscure event, the crucifixion of a religious leader in Judea, reached our day from that day, those rumours, we may rely upon it, would have been conflicting. Each section of the unhappy dispersion would have had its version of Jesus and of the Cross—without a sequel.

But they did not disperse. They reassembled, and in a spirit altogether new. Then after a while they did indeed part, but to preach one message, to confess and glorify one Lord. And the one solution of all this is—the Resurrection. Every other explanation is a violent process; it either ignores the despair and separation of the disciples at first, or the completeness and grandeur of their moral *and mental* revolution, so prompt, decisive, and unanimous.

Verse 25. *So the other disciples began to say to him, We have seen the Lord.*

Surely they went to seek him with the news, perhaps that very night, for probably the presence of the Lord with them that evening was brief, as it seems to have been on other recorded occasions. The one Apostle who did not yet know of the mighty joy must have been an object of strong and loving interest and sympathy to his friends. If they had been tempted before to be impatient when he withdrew, they would be more than patient now; for what can so fully calm the discords of the soul in itself, and open it out in unselfish sympathy, as the possession of a great spiritual joy? This now indeed these men had. They knew Jesus Risen; they knew that He had given them His peace; they knew that He had died for them, and was alive for evermore.

"He *that believeth* shall not *make haste*" (Isa. xxviii. 16). An eagerness for religious opinions, for religious truths, which is at all harsh or bitter, is not seldom due to uneasiness, not to conviction. It is one thing to be unwaveringly and entirely in earnest, another thing to be heated. Peter, John, Nathanael, and the rest would not be hard upon Thomas because he had not been with them. Full of their unspeakably glad discovery, rich in the ample possession of such a Saviour, they can only have longed with sympathetic graciousness that their friend should share it to the full.

Meanwhile, the witness would be as positive as it was kind. *We have seen the Lord;* an absolute fact. *We,* not others; *have seen,* not guessed or dreamed; *the Lord,* identical and immortal in His love and glory.

So they would bear witness; lovingly, positively, and as men who were fresh from the special benediction of the Risen One. And they were persons with whom Thomas had long been familiar, and whose concurrence of witness must to him have been impressive, for they were no mere copies of each other.

Yet all this witnessing wholly, or nearly wholly, failed. It was continued, repeated; ἔλεγον. But Thomas met it with an outspoken scepticism and refusal. Unless his own senses should assure him, *he would never believe,* οὐ μὴ πιστεύσω.

He was very, very wrong. The whole narrative, and the whole Scripture, illustrate this. In Scripture the evidence of the senses is never slighted, never said to be illusory. But it is shewn to be not the only evidence. Adequate testimony may fully take its place, even when a soul is in the question.

It was wrong; and yet who, that knows his own human heart, will say that it was unnatural? Who, that knows how violently *self*, in any of its forms, can warp reason or affection, when once self is allowed to have its way, will sit in superior judgment upon Thomas? For surely it was this subtle subjective obstacle that held him. If, as is so likely, grief had developed a certain gloomy pride of isolation, and then upon it had come in this news of the great joy found by those whom he had left in a spirit like his own, can we wonder if for the time the very thought of their certainty and happiness embittered and hardened his own resolve to doubt and to differ? A subtle sense of mortification may well have tinged the words: *Unless I see in His hands the print of the nails, and insert my finger into the print of the nails, and insert my hand into His side, I will never believe.*

Many strange but actual workings of human nature, in the absence of the peace and love of God, seem to be remarkably illustrated by the acts and words of Thomas in his gloom.

Perhaps we have in him an example of many minds among those which now doubt or reject the Gospel. Self (to use the word in the sense not of mere vanity, or shallow self-importance, but rather in that of a morbid introspection) often stands more than the doubter suspects between him and conviction. The proof which is really good for another is good for him, in itself. But it is seen distorted, for it is seen askance. We need not live long to find out how, in the practical affairs of common life, personal peculiarities interfere with apparently self-evidently beneficial and just courses of action. Even so, in the microcosm within us, reason and conscience have often to fight a hard, and often a losing, battle with some purely irrational opposition of unregenerate self. How happy it is when that self is subdued, as the soul of Thomas was subdued, by the revelation of Jesus Christ as He is; living, loving, slain and risen again, my Lord, and my God!

Verse 26. *And after eight days again the disciples were indoors, and Thomas with them.*

"After eight days," a full week. We are left almost entirely uninformed as to the life of the disciples "between times" during the Forty Days. We see them, as it were, only under the illumination of their Lord's presence; He goes, and the shadow falls over them for the time. So we do not know how that week was passed, only that it must assuredly have been a week of great, though private, gladness. "The fear of the Jews" must have been strangely neutralized by the consciousness of the victory and life of the Lord Jesus, while yet the disciples appear to have kept silence about it beyond their own circle—surely in consequence of a command from Him. On the other hand, their enemies seem to have been quite satisfied, so to speak, with the disappearance of the Master, and to have meditated no assault on the disciples. Whatever the mystery of the disappearance of Jesus was to Caiaphas and his fellows, *He had disappeared;* He had become at the most a spectre to them; and so manifest was the inferiority of His followers' power to move and to attract, that the Sanhedrin, it would seem, fairly dismissed the thought of them from their minds.

So the week passed, outwardly undisturbed, as far as we know or can guess. But *within* the little company, great was the stir. This obstinate doubter—this stubborn rejecter of the multifold witness to the great fact of joy—what was to be done in view of him? Again and again they would attack him with a loving siege; but the subtle influence ruled Thomas still. He would not believe.

It was a severe lesson to them all, though a lesson richly blessed, no doubt. For all their after ministry it must have taught them much;

K

it must have pressed home on them for all time the incapacity of man to set free by his own act and word his brother's soul; the weakness of mere evidences, however convincing in the abstract, to sway the heart and will without the eternal grace; the possibilities of doubt in another over what was to themselves so self-evident, and about which they were so greatly happy. Let us learn our lesson from theirs; we shall surely need it, sooner or later, if we at all attempt to bear witness for the Lord.

Meantime their words, though they had not convinced Thomas, had told upon him. Another "First Day" at length arrived, bringing back in new realization all the circumstances of the former "First Day"; and now Thomas was with them.

That week, we may be sure, had not shaken the faith of "the other disciples." Their witness to the Risen One was not less positive because their brother refused it. And even this must have told upon him. The sight of their certainty would touch, however invisibly, his convictions. The sight of their happiness must have moved his longings, even when he most freely indulged his own self-centred gloom.

They were indoors again. Thomas, in this state betwixt doubt and desire, was with them, ready, humanly speaking, to be swayed either way by what might happen. Can we doubt that, if nothing had happened, or if anything unconvincing had happened, his whole mind would have turned to a distrust more positive than ever? Could we suppose for a moment so monstrous a thing as that his brethren had devised some illusion to work on his imagination, he was just in the mood to look it through and through, and to be irrevocably confirmed in his denial by the detection of the slightest unreality.

But now what happened?

Verse 26. *Jesus comes, while the doors were fastened, and took His stand in the midst and said, Peace be unto you. Then He says to Thomas, Bring your finger hither, and see My hands, and bring your hand, and insert it into My side, and do not become unbelieving, but believing.*

It is vain to try any elaborate "word-painting" here. The wonderful scene of mercy and joy stands out before us. There are the disciples, perhaps in the act of some fresh effort of reasoning and witness addressed to the stubborn personality of the doubter, each trying his own way; there is Thomas, perhaps more than ever, to all appearance, argumentative, critical, resolved. Then, on a sudden, with the same miracle of silent entrance, the great Reasoner, the faithful Witness, Himself is there once more; JESUS, bringing the brief and mighty logic and demonstration of Himself revealed. We see Him extend His holy and deathless hands, each showing the cleft of the huge nail; we see Him move His robe, and disclose the yet wider and deeper chasm of the spear, that great wound which only St John records.

There they were displayed once more, these marks of the identity of Jesus as the Lamb that was slain. The Lord displayed them then, that we might believe on Him as such for ever. We may or may not be permitted to see them with our eyes hereafter, but to faith they are indelible; to the love which sees through tears of joy that Saviour so slain, they are in sight for evermore.

> For ever here my rest shall be,
>   Close to Thy bleeding side;
> This all my hope and all my plea,
>   For me the Saviour died.
>
> How blest are they who still abide,
> Close shelter'd in Thy bleeding side;
> Who life and strength from thence derive,
> And by Thee move, and in Thee live.

So there, in the lamplight, Thomas had his will. Definitely and unmistakably he there saw the Lord risen, and the marks of His slaughter. And he heard the voice of the Risen One; it addressed him articulately and personally; it recited with strange precision the challenge which he had made so stoutly to his brethren. He was to do the very thing; to come close, to touch, to insert, to feel, and to believe.

Whether Thomas actually "brought thither his finger" we do not know. Probably he did, with tenderest reverence. But it is possible that he did not, so self-evident was the *sight*. His own eyes, those unready eyes, now saw his own unmistakable Master, and the *contact* may have been almost deprecated. Certainly in the Lord's answer to the disciple's confession, only his sight is referred to.

Verse 28. *Thomas answered and said unto Him, My Lord and my God. Jesus says to him, Because you have seen Me, Thomas, you have believed; happy such as saw not and believed.*

The sequel of the interview is not recorded. As in every other Resurrection appearance, except only the incident at Emmaus, and the Ascension, we do not read any detail of the Lord's *departure*. That night He may have stayed with them, to speak of the things of the kingdom, or He may have left them as silently as He came—left them to their now completed and united joy.

But for us, as we read and think, He "goes out no more." There for ever is He, this same Jesus; and there is the subdued, happy doubter, gazing on Him, confessing Him as his Lord and his God. JESUS and Thomas are immortally present before us in that upper room, "that we, too, may believe that Jesus is the Christ, the Son of God, and that we too, believing, may have life in His name."

THOMAS is there, in his confession: *My Lord and my God*. Strange sound from those lips! The perplexed and perplexing sceptic has come to utter a confession whose glorious fulness, and also whose personal application ("*my* Lord"), surpass even Peter's at Cæsarea Philippi, when the Father revealed to him the Son. "My GOD"—words impossible to explain away, for they were addressed obviously to Jesus direct, and they meant no less than proper Godhead, for they were uttered by an Israelite.

So Thomas confessed Him, and received Him. Doubt was gone, reserve broken, the soul quite released from the sullen wish to keep its old isolated position in sorrowful pride. He is one with his brethren now, and they shall know it; for he has found in Jesus Risen all his desire, all his joy.

It is no unique case. How often the most positive denials have been exchanged for the very simplest faith! St Augustine is a memorable example, not to speak of Saul of Tarsus. And many a later illustration of the same phenomenon may be quoted. Never shall I forget the authentic experience of an aged man, refined and cultured, and a resolved Socinian, who had always maintained that he had never seen Priestley really answered. Late in the long evening of his life (he died at ninety-two) his doctor one day found him, much to his surprise, dropping tears over his Bible. He had seen a new light. He had met with a Biblical phrase never noticed before, or, however, never thought of before; *The blood of Jesus Christ His Son cleanseth us from all sin.* He too, like Thomas, after many asseverations of unbelief, reaching over many more days than eight, had seen THE LORD, and bowed before Him, in the light of the living relation between the virtue of the atoning blood and the eternal Nature of the Crucified.

And then, in this immortal chamber scene, JESUS is there. He meets the confession of His disciple—how quietly, how divinely! There is no word of caution; there is no "See thou do it not; worship God." There is rather a gentle reproof that the faith so expressed had not come sooner: "Not till sight have you believed; happy such as believe without sight." Yes, Jesus, the meek and lowly, who made Himself of no reputation, accepts this ascription of Deity as calmly as a king, born to the throne, and long upon it, accepts the ascription of loyalty from a humble subject. He only bends to His Apostle in loving censure for his past reluctance, and then gives, by anticipation, a royal blessing to—ourselves.

Happy such as saw not, and believed. Not, Happy such as believed without a reason, without a ground, but, Happy they who did not create out of themselves reasons against belief. Such, surely, is the point of this precious last Beatitude. It refers to the special difficulty of Thomas, to that obstacle to faith which individualism, which self (for this it was assuredly), had raised in the way of his accepting evidence altogether adequate. The truth had looked like a phantom to him because seen through that mist. Happy they, says the Lord, who are free from that. Happy they, oh how happy, whatever else they see or do not see, who see the witness borne to Jesus with the simplicity of a soul which seeks not self's way, but pardon, and holiness, and heaven; which indulges no jealous comparison of self with others, and allows no restless, morbid discouragement to come from that quarter. That soul grudges no privilege, experience, freedom, power to other believers; but, in the unspeakably happy consciousness of the reception for itself of such a Saviour on His own terms, believes indeed, rests on Him, in perfect simplicity and with perfect reason. It demands no peculiar and privileged demonstration, for it needs none. It is happy, it is assured, it loves, it obeys; for it is emancipated from those subtle influences of the protean spirit of self which alone can make the evidence of the Gospel pages and the glad witness of already blessed believers unconvincing.

How would the released and adoring Apostle, standing free at length from self, at the feet of Jesus, exhort us, if we could hear him, to listen every day to this divine assurance of the blessedness of believing, and, for that purpose, to use every day the precious written record; or (ver. 31) *these things have been written that we may believe that Jesus is the Christ, the Son of God, and that, believing, we may have life in His name.*

> I would go from pole to pole
> To behold my risen Lord;
> But content thyself, my soul,
> Listen to thy Saviour's word:
> " They who Me by faith receive,
> Without seeing who believe,
> Trust My word and therein rest,
> They abundantly are blest."
>
> Moravian Hymn-book.

IX

THE NIGHT ON THE LAKE.

WE approach the last Chapter of the Gospel according to St John. As before, we open our study with a paraphrastic version.

After these things Jesus manifested Himself again to the disciples upon (beside) the sea of Tiberias; and He manifested Himself thus. There were together Simon Peter and Thomas, whose name means Twin, and Nathanaël, from Cana in Galilee, and the two sons of Zebedee, and other two of His disciples. Simon Peter says to them, I am going to fish. They say to him, We are coming with you too. They went out, and embarked in the boat; and that night they took nothing. But when daybreak was now come, Jesus came and stood on the beach (ἔστη εἰ τὸν αἰγιαλόν); the disciples however did not know that it is Jesus. So Jesus says to them, Children, you have not any fish? They answered Him, No. Then He said to them, Throw your net towards the right side of the boat, and you will find. So they threw; and now strength ailed them (οὐκέτι ἴσχυσαν) *to draw, such was the quantity of fish. So that disciple whom Jesus loved said to Peter, It is the Lord. So Simon Peter, hearing that it is the Lord, girded on his outer coat, for he was naked, and threw himself into the sea. The other disciples now came with the smaller boat; for they were not far from the land, only about two hundred cubits off, dragging the netful of fish. So when they had disembarked, they see a coalfire laid, and a dish of fish set at it, and a loaf. Jesus says to them, Bring some of the fish which you have just taken. Simon Peter got up (into the smaller boat), and pulled the net up on the land, quite full of large fish, a hundred and fifty-three. And although they were so many, the net had not been torn.*

Verse 1. *After these things.* The interval is not specified. It may have been now very near the day of the Ascension. But is it not more likely that it was not long after the confession of Thomas—say within the first three weeks of the Forty Days? One consideration speaks strongly for this; I mean, that the full and solemn restoration of Peter to the apostolic pastorate took place on this occasion. Surely this would not be delayed long after the Resurrection.

This appearance, we observe again, is in Galilee. Here is one of the places where St John incidentally, and as it were covertly, agrees with the other Gospels. They record the command to the Apostles to meet the Lord in Galilee; he does not. But more fully than any of them John records the fact of their doing what was commanded. Now the removal of the Apostles to Galilee came almost to a certainty soon after the Resurrection, soon after the close of the Passover-time. It is unlikely that anything but Passover obligations would keep them lingering in Jerusalem at all in face of that command and promise.

There then, in Galilee, they found themselves once more. In Galilee took place this blessed interview. In Galilee, with a company of some five hundred others, they met Jesus at that unnamed mountain (was it Tabor, or was it Hermon?) where He had appointed them (Matt. xxviii. 16; 1 Cor. xv. 6). There very probably they saw Him many other times not recorded. And thence, before six weeks were over, they returned again to the city, to the upper room, and to the glorious farewell on the top of Olivet.

A partial veil, a haze of mysterious light, is

drawn across this holy and most memorable period, the Forty Days. Notes of time here are scarce; intervals are wide and empty. How different is this from the season just previous, the Passion Week in particular, where the diary is so full, so crowded! Ὀπτανόμενος διὰ ἡμερῶν τεσσαράκοντα, *Seen as by glimpses, at intervals, during forty days*, is St Luke's account (Acts i. 3) of the Lord Jesus now. Separate appearances are, specially by St John, recorded with minute care; only the *dis*appearances, except at Emmaus and in the Ascension, are never recorded. But the intervals are left without a conjecture, without a hint. There is no legendary unreality about this. Rather, under the alleged conditions, it is deeply truth-like.

At some time then undefined, but perhaps within a fortnight of the Resurrection, we find some at least of the disciples returned to Galilee. Seven are mentioned; but plainly more than seven were near, or it would not be noticed specially that these seven were "together."

There they were, in their old haunts, at their old work. We cannot know for certain under what conditions they were at that work. Had Peter returned to his home, as home? Had James and John rejoined their father in his fishery? It would seem incredible. They were in Galilee because the Risen Lord had bid them go there; and for the express purpose of "seeing Him." And He had already spoken words to them which showed with abundant clearness that their life's work was to be labour for the souls of sinners in His Name, and was soon to begin. With such a prospect they could not possibly go back, in the old way, to boats and nets.

So we may think of them as returned to Galilee and the Lake filled with the expectation of Jesus, but meanwhile not therefore forbidding themselves a sojourn, a lodging, under old roofs and amidst old occupations. Their Lord's company and teaching in the past, while it had always tended to disengage them from *the bondage* of the things of time, had never for a moment tended to break their sympathy with the common life, and work, and affections of men. And they were all, in all probability, as we have already remarked, in the full vigour of young manhood, contemporaries of their Master. To await Him was blessed; but to await Him in inaction would have been for them unnatural.

How familiar to them, and yet how strangely different too, must the scenes and the life have been! Little more than a quarter of a year had passed since last they were there. But those few weeks were the turning-point of the history of man. A great change had come over even external conditions. There was no more the old eager and excited following about of a wonderful Leader. No longer did ever-growing Galilean multitudes throng to hear and to watch, and clamour to proclaim Him King Messiah. All this had now passed into total silence. For the time, perhaps, in the common thought of Galilee, His name had been already classed with those of Theudas and the Gaulonite Judas, exposed and ruined aspirants to the honours of Messiah. All was silent now on the mount where the Man of Nazareth had taught, and quiet in the sunny streets where He had healed the sick people, and very solitary on that eastern shore of the Lake where He had expelled the fallen spirits, and had fed the multitudes arranged in their "parterres" ($\pi\rho\alpha\sigma\iota\alpha\acute{\iota}$, Mark vi. 40) of hundreds and fifties. Many a Galilean heart which had never seen below the radiant surface of the life of Jesus must yet have felt the profound difference. Air and earth and waters were the same; a glorious scene, glorious even now amidst comparative desertion. But the wonderful presence of the Prophet was gone, and gone (for the popular mind) into such a blank, such a gloom. Faint rumours of the

Resurrection may have reached the Galilean villages, apart from anything said by the inner circle of disciples; but even these would be mingled with the Jewish lie (Matt. xxviii. 15) which denied it. And we gather that the disciples themselves were not a little reticent about the Resurrection beyond their own company till Pentecost arrived; so reticent indeed that their witness then evidently broke as a great surprise upon the people. The thoughtful Christian may surely find in this one of the "truth-likenesses" of the Gospel narratives.

But to these disciples themselves meanwhile, in the secret soul, and in the private conversation, the familiar scenery would present another and far different change. Outwardly all was hushed, and as it were motionless; inwardly all was glowing and moving with new and glorious while infinitely solemn life. They had seen the Lord. They knew Him as alive for evermore. As yet doubtless they had taken in but little comparatively of the divine import of the Resurrection; but, at least—they knew the Lord as Risen! The mangled Victim of the Roman cross was alive, alive eternally; sure to triumph now in the great issues of His will and work, sure to be glorified, sure to save, lead, raise and glorify *them*. However reticent about it, they must have begun already in their old Galilee to live the life of heaven. They were being already transfigured from the earthly to the heavenly mind. The glories of their native land and air would now be to them fair parables of the resurrection world, of an inheritance reserved in heaven. Above all, their thoughts now would be, as they were to be for ever, filled to overflowing with Jesus and His glory. The sight of Him in His Resurrection must indeed have been soul-possessing; the first deep draught drawn by mortal hearts at the unfathomed fountain of the absolute and finished redemption from guilt, sin, death, which is, and is to come, in Jesus Christ.

Thank God, that fountain is yet springing up unto life eternal, that discovery is ever making. For innumerable hearts to-day (and are not ours among them?) earth, in all its regions and climates, is lighted up from heaven,[1] "because Jesus died and rose again"; "because the Son of God is come, and hath given us an understanding, and we are in Him, the True" (1 John v. 20).

In this Galilean scenery and sojourn, then, the Lord again manifested Himself to the disciples beside (ἐπί) the Tiberias Lake.

[1] See Appendix ii.

And He manifested Himself thus.

Verse 2. *There were together* the aforementioned seven. Four then of the Eleven were absent. We have no hint of a reason why. But both the mention of the number and the absence of anxious explanation fall perfectly in with this wonderful photograph of details by one who saw.

They were together, very probably in Capernaum, in Peter's house, waiting for their absent but promised Lord, waiting it may be for several days. And now some untold passing thing suggests, amidst the expectancy, their old occupation. The water is close by, and there lie the πλοῖον and the πλοιάριον of the house, the boat and its tender, and the sky and the lake promise well. And in the thought of embarkation there would be no discord with thoughts of Jesus. In that boat He had sate; He had taught from its bench; He had slept (Mark iv. 38) with His head upon its cushion.

So the men, being together, go out together to their old acts and habits, feeling very possibly, just as young men now might feel, the curious interest of returning for a while to a disused exercise of strength and skill. They take the two boats, the larger and the lesser, of which more hereafter. All probably entered the boat, and worked it together through the night; and all probably in the morning transferred themselves at last to the tender, except Peter, who had first reached the shore through the water.[1]

We watch the party which embarked: Peter, still leading with the spirit and word of enterprise; Thomas, the self-conscious and self-asserting doubter no more, but willingly "together" with the rest; Nathanael (no born fisherman), the guileless and genuine Israelite, the man of secret prayer; John, the beloved, already finding it habitual to be at Peter's side; James, his brother, first of the company to go to the Lord through death, as John the last; and the other nameless two, whom we may, if we will, suppose to be Andrew and his fellow Bethsaidan Philip. They were indeed together; in the house, on the water, and at length again on the other shore; and never again in the sense of inner union were they to be apart; working together on the world's tide with the net of souls, and sitting down at last together on the immortal strand around their glorified Lord Jesus.

It is of the essence of the Gospel to unite where it touches. It is obvious, as we saw

---

[1] I owe this explanation of the probable circumstances to a kind communication from Mr P. Vernon Smith.

above (p. 123), that the first disciples must have been scattered, in shame, disgust, suspicion, if the Lord had not risen from the grave. The Gospels show them in the act, as we trace the walk to Emmaus, and the conduct of Thomas. But a Saviour risen again (and HE *is* the Gospel) is indeed a magnetic force to draw round Himself, and to draw to, nay, as it were, into one another, the utmost variety of human souls. A personal and recognized interest in His merits, and experience of His presence and His power, as we realize that ours is but one harmonious instance among countless others of the "reception of Christ Jesus the Lord" (Col. ii. 6)—this does indeed draw hearts together. And we may be very sure that this sense of a blessed community will be intensified, not chilled, by the intensity of the individual's sense of peace and power in Christ.

Verse 3. *Simon Peter says to them, I am going to fish.* So St John records the simple words with which that memorable night's labour was begun, and then he tells us how they stepped into the boat, and then how the spring evening and midnight were spent, as it seemed, in vain. *That night they took nothing; and daybreak was now come.* How brief and reserved it all is, till Jesus appears! So it is ever in the evangelical narrative. With Jesus present, details come thick and fast—details which manifest HIM. Here, the night is recorded in one line. We should like to know all about it; what was the look of the dark water, and the brightness of the stars above, and the stirring of the air, and the sounds on flood and shore. We should like to understand what filled the hearts of those seven men that night; whether they were fairly bent upon their work, and so quite alive to delays and disappointments, or whether expectations of a far higher sort were strong enough to let them "ply their watery task" inattentively. The former alternative is more probable, for the record seems to show them at early morning so unexpectant of the Lord's coming to them just then that it needed the miracle to awaken them to consciousness of Him. They act, as we then see them, just like men fatigued and bewildered by long and real but fruitless effort.

But as to all details, inward and outward alike, we are left without the least certainty. Imagination shows us the two spots upon the dusky waters, under the aërial gloom of the deep midnight. It lets us hear the fishermen as they call to one another, to enquire, encourage, or direct, in the tone and phrase of Galilee.

Yet all this is mere reverie, and we do well to remember it.

But it is truth, not imagination, that bids us see in that fruitless night of toil, followed by so blessed a morrow, not only a precious narrative of real events but a living message of strength to the Christian man in the hour of trial, of delay, of seemingly unrequited labour for the Lord; and a living message, too, to the Christian Church, upon the deep dark waters of sin and time, waiting for the eternal morning, and the great ingathering, and the manifested Saviour;

> While night
> Invests the sea, and wished morn delays.

Let us lay it thankfully to heart.

X

JOY IN THE MORNING.

So the seven disciples went out for their evening's fishing, and spent that summer night in vain efforts on the lake. *And that night they took nothing.* No doubt many a well-known favourable place was tried, now the nearer now the further shore, the deeper and the shallower waters. Most of them were experienced fishermen, and they were at work where the prey was then, as now, abundant. But "that night they took nothing."

It was not an unprecedented disappointment. Some three years before they had passed a similar night (Luke v.), the night which ushered in the day when some of them received from their Friend and Teacher the call which changed their whole after-life:—"Master (Ἐπιστάτα), we have toiled all the night and taken nothing; nevertheless at Thy word I will let down the net." There was *that* precedent at least to be remembered; and perhaps there were other occasions when they had borne the burthens of a fruitless night, though the emphasis with which these two experiences are recorded seems to say that such a night was not an ordinary incident. It was as it were part and parcel with the miraculously fruitful morning.

Certainly it was a providential preparation for it. The true Son of Man (Psa. viii. 4) ruled the waters and their tribes all that night through. "The fishes of the sea, and whatsoever walketh through the paths of the sea"—of them we read in that Messianic oracle that they are part of His dominion. Let us remember, as most certainly St John means us to do, that it was He who that night *willed* the hours of frustration and failure. The providence and decree of Jesus Christ deliberately and effectually disappointed His dear disciples' hopes and efforts. The weary hands, the aching eyes, the baffled skill, He had to do with it all. It was the Lord.

It is well worth our while to bear this in mind for our own help. Not seldom the servant of God is called upon to use his best skill and strength *apparently* in vain; to labour unmistakably in vain as regards immediate successes. Not always indeed; in many cases not very often; but certainly, upon the whole, not very seldom. Such experiences should always lead us to self-searching, to see what *in us* may perhaps be the reason of failure, in our spirit toward others, or towards the Lord, or in our ways and means of labour. But when, as in His presence, we may humbly believe that in these respects His will is being done in us and by us, and yet we seem to "spend our strength for nought," then let us remember the night spent on the Galilean lake, and be reassured. We shall yet find that the disappointment is, in providence, as much a blessing as the success is; in fact, a part of the success, its prelude and preface.

Could the Seven have foreseen, however dimly, their Master's presence the next morning, and realized, however faintly, that He was in those dark hours already acting upon them and around them, would it not have lightened all the burthen indescribably? All vexation would have vanished out of the delay, simply because of their consciousness of the life, the will, the love of their Saviour and their God.

It would seem however that they had no such forecast.

Verse 4. *But when daybreak was now come, Jesus came and stood on the beach* (the eastern beach, as we gather from the evident solitude of the place); *the disciples however did not know that it is Jesus.* No; they did not know it, even John did not know it, till the miracle, the σημεῖον, was fairly done. We gather that the undefined transfiguration of our Lord's appearance, so often hinted at in the Resurrection narratives, was here also operating to delay their recognition. But we may also infer that their minds as well as eyes were at fault; they were not on the look-out to see Him; or surely the first sight of any solitary figure on the beach would have at once suggested the question, Is it not the Lord?

We can do little more than note this peculiar unconsciousness of the Apostles. Like other instances of their oblivion or "slowness" of heart, it speaks truth and fact by its very unlikelihood *à priori*, and by the perfect simplicity of the record of it. It is precisely unlike an invention. If an invention, it would be of course the invention of a later generation, when these fishermen were already viewed with the deepest reverence as the builders and rulers of the Christian community. Would an artificial picture of their conduct, drawn at such a date, have taken the line which the Gospels do take, the line of freest description and criticism of their slowness and fallibility of perception?

The thoroughly human, imperfect, provincial character and conduct attributed as a fact to the Apostles in the Gospels has thus a precious value as internal evidence of the genuineness of the record. Again and again be it said, the picture is not a composition; it is a photograph. It is not an ideal; it is life.

So here we have not a company of hardly human beings, seen in "the light that never was on sea or land"; their every faculty always awake to Christ and to heaven. We have a group of men, engrossed for the time with the expectations and disappointments of common work, toiling on from hour to hour, very tired no doubt by the morning, their senses all strained and aching, bewildered and forgetting.

When it was dawn, then, in the pale rising light, where the eastward hills rise ridge over ridge towards Trachonitis, throwing their deep and misty shadows towards the water, then and there the Risen *Jesus stood upon the beach, came and stood upon the beach,* the αἰγιαλός, the pebbly or sandy margin of the crystal water. How had He spent the night? Had He walked upon the deep as long ago, though now unseen? Or had He been traversing in the quiet hours the scenes which in the days of His mortality He had frequented with His blessed presence? How total our ignorance is before such a question! The reality, the literality, of the life of the Risen One we know; blessed be the name of His Father. We know that our Redeemer lived, and liveth. But of the conditions of that life of His literal and bodily Resurrection we know, in detail, almost nothing. It is enough, however. The holy narratives lift the veil high enough to show us a Saviour present, accessible, identical, perfect God, perfect Man; alive in all His love and power, and saying to us, "Ye shall live also."

He stood upon the shore, a solitary figure, seen over "the wan water," a hundred yards or so from the boat. Peter, and John, and their fellows, could well see Him, but none of them recognized Him. Busy perhaps with some last haul of the empty net, or listless and inobservant with fatigue, *they knew not that it is Jesus.*

Verse 5. *So Jesus says to them, Children you have not any fish?* Μή τι προσφάγιον ἔχετε; The μή implies the supposition that they had *not* taken anything.

Παιδία, *Children.* The word is used almost as "Lads" might be used now, importing (as some similar phrases amongst our poor people do) only neighbourhood and friendliness, not necessarily a paternal superiority. We may observe that it is not "*My* children;" for scarcely ever, if ever, does the Saviour—at least in the days of His flesh—address His followers as *His children* at all; John xiii. 33 is not an exception.[1] They are *His brethren.* "He is not ashamed" (hard as it sometimes is, for joy, to believe it) "to call us brethren" (Heb. ii. 11); His Father's children. This, however, is by the way. The word παιδία here would be understood as merely a kindly expression on the part of the unknown visitor.

St Chrysostom, who tends as an expositor to a very simple and even homely explanation of details, thinks that Jesus may have put this question meaning to speak as *an intending purchaser* (ὡς μέλλων τι ὠνεῖσθαι παρ' αὐτῶν). It may be so. But the other suggestion seems to fit more naturally into the scene — that the question was as from a man looking with friendly interest on what was manifestly a moment of fruitless toil. Faint and disheartened those boatmen may well have *looked*, as they trailed the slack net. *So you have had no success, then?*

Thus the voice came from the shore, audible

---

[1] In Heb. ii. 33 the "children" are *God's* children entrusted to His Son. See the context.

and articulate as it always is over water. *They answered Him, No;* the brief reply of tired men.

Verse 6. *Then He said to them, Throw your net on the right side of the boat, and you will find.*

The young men acted at once upon the words. No doubt there was a spell upon them; for when JESUS speaks it is more than words. But the supernatural spell acted, as is almost always the case, through nature. Partly the non-resistance of fatigue, partly the faint hope of success by any means, partly and perhaps chiefly the thought that the stranger from his standpoint might see a cause for his confident words which they could not see—these may have been the motives. Possibly too there came over them a vague and indefinable sense (we all know what that is like) of a previous occurrence of the whole event; each step was in the footmarks of the past.

So they threw; and now strength failed them to draw, such was the quantity of fish. Here, by the way, is an incidental touch of accuracy. This inability to draw in a net which though full was not extraordinarily full (ver. 11) shows that the hands were very tired.

What the Five said and did we do not know; the narrator can think just now only of Peter and himself.

Wonderful pair of friends! More and more, in the narrative, we find them, as we saw above (p. 18), together. Essentially different in natural character, they are now however drawn irrevocably side to side. Each has a brother who is also a chief Apostle; but Peter and John are somehow more than brothers to each other now. We shall see yet more striking proof of this before the Gospel closes; but let us here note the fact. And let us remember how affectingly all these records of the loving union of Peter and John, *written by John,* answer that shallow and trivial insinuation of the sceptic that this chapter was written with the poor purpose of making Peter less and John more prominent than before.

And now these two men, drawn thus together, made thus for ever one in the love of Jesus, go on to act, each in his way; John sees, and Peter moves.

Verse 7. *So that disciple whom Jesus loved says to Peter, It is the Lord.* He saw that it was Jesus. Probably his *eyes* saw nothing new; it was the same figure standing there, the same just visible face. But the σημεῖον, the sign-wonder, waked his soul to conscious insight with his eyes; and he knew who it was—THE LORD.

In passing we may notice once more that title, as sweet as it is reverently solemn, which after the Resurrection seems to become the habitual designation of the Risen One, THE LORD. Let us note the word, as thus employed by the beloved one, by John; by him who delights to tell us, with holy simplicity, that Jesus had been pleased to admit him to a peculiar personal intimacy. Yet even for John, Jesus is THE LORD. And will it not be ever thus with us also, as we grow in knowledge and in love of Him? Intimacy between sinner and sinner may often lead to diminution of respect; intimacy between the redeemed sinner and JESUS CHRIST, the more He is known as He is, can only lead to a deeper, a more unreserved, reverence and adoration. Dost thou very dearly love Him? Has He very wonderfully made manifest to thee His love for thee? Then surely by thee above all others He will be known and worshipped as THE LORD.

Thus John beheld Jesus. He saw the Son of God. He was conscious of His Person and Presence, which but for that insight were but the person and presence of a chance passer-by upon the lonely beach.

So Simon Peter, hearing that it is the Lord, girded on his outer coat, for he was naked, and threw himself into the lake.

He heard who it was; he did not look, it seems, to verify the hearing. The tone of John

M

spoke for itself, and this was what, for Peter, brought the soul to look, to see the Son of God. Are we not reminded that often, very often, the calm, happy certainty shown by some beloved and trusted friend with regard to the Saviour's life, and love, and power, proves to the soul (perhaps in some hour of perplexity or bitterness) its own truthfulness? It shines out direct, an evidence of Christianity, a manifestation of Christ. "He knoweth that he saith true, that ye may believe."

Peter now acts in his own way upon the words of John. Two sides of his remarkable character come out; an almost impetuous devotion to his Master, and a most keen consciousness of his personal unworthiness to be in his Master's presence. He was naked, γυμνός. That is to say, in all probability, as frequent usage illustrates the meaning, he was half clad, wearing nothing but an under tunic. However, he was so attired that he could not choose to appear so before "the Lord." And he wraps the outer coat around him, the ἐπενδύτης, the large overcoat for storms and cold nights. And *he girt it well round him*, διεζώσατο. It was a simple but true expression of profound reverence, the same spirit which had once (Luke v. 8) prompted him to cry, "Depart from me." But that spirit was more enlightened now, for Peter's resistless impulse now is—to draw near. He knew now, not that Jesus was less awfully holy, but that His very holiness made it necessary, and blessed, for Peter to be quite near Him. And it is so still. Jesus Christ would not be THE SAVIOUR were He not infinitely holy. But He *is* the Saviour, and being so He must be actually approached, actually touched, by the sinner who so much wants Him. And the sinner now, like Peter of old, as he comes and touches, will remember both truths—that indeed His name is Holy, but also that to come actually *to Him*, to nothing intermediate, but to Him, is not rashness but obedience, not presumption but salvation.

He threw himself into the lake, leaving John, and the five others, to step, it would seem, from the boat into the tender, anchor the boat, and, in the tender, haul the net to shore. Peter threw himself in, and crossed the hundred yards of water, swimming and wading (we seem to see the silver spray of the plunge, and the eager passage), to find himself as soon as he can be at the feet of the Prince of Life. Yes, he must be as near as possible, and that as soon as possible, to Him whom he had denied a few weeks ago, over and over, but who had nevertheless gone on to die for him and rise again.

Verse 8. What that first moment's interview was, we are not told. The whole group of seven were now on land. The five had assisted John to bring boats and net to the shore; and then apparently at once, without hauling *up* the net, but leaving it fast to the boat, full of its struggling prize, they had stepped out and so drew near the Lord.

Verse 9. And now, in the solitary place, beside Him, they see a meal already preparing. A fire, a coal fire, was already there; and beside its ruddy flame fish was set for eating, and the bread was ready. Manifestly there was mystery, if not miracle, in this provision, and He near whom they stood had something to teach them by it. Was it not the lesson of His independence of them, and yet care for them, and fellowship with them? It was this at least. And now He bids them add their own to His—their own, which however was His also; for what they had just caught He had by His will given them. They were to *bring it*, however.

Verse 10. *Jesus says to them, Bring some of the fish which you have just taken.* *Simon Peter got up* (from the beach into the tender-boat), *and,* standing there, *pulled up the net quite full of large fish.* And Peter counted the number over; we seem to hear his voice as he "tells the tale"; a distinct and definite report, no round number, *one hundred and fifty-three*. It was a large haul for that one cast-net; *and yet, although they were so many, the net had not been torn.*

So Peter's work, and his account of it, is done; and then again the solemn reticence of the Lord is broken, and He calls them to a meal around Him.

The details of ver. 12 and those which follow upon it we must consider in another chapter. All I attempt to do now, as we shut the Book once more, is to recall the reality of the blessed scene. We look on it again; the sun comes up over the hills, and turns the grey waters into gold. And there—look along the shore from where we stand—there is that group around the flame under the steep slope that borders the beach. Eight persons; seven mortal men, sitting down to their food, and in the midst of them One who is also, and supremely, Man; visible, palpable, no illusion; the risen, the ever-living Jesus.

Let us turn away thankful, if we have again indeed seen HIM; Him living then, and therefore "alive for evermore"; alive now, loving, watching, present, now. Well do I remember, though long years have passed, how at a time of great mental and spiritual trial I found, by God's great mercy, peculiar help in just this way from this very scene, as it invited me to realize afresh this mysterious but actual personal life and presence of Jesus Christ.

There, in the sight of Him, is peace. To see and know Him living, living after He had for us "poured out His soul unto death," is the solution of doubts, the banishment of fears, the conquest of passions, the strength of the soul. From amidst that group of disciples He still says, to us to-day, "Fear not; you indeed are mortal, sinful, feeble, helpless; but I am the First and the Last; I am the Living One. I was dead, but behold I am alive for ever, alive for you, with you, in you, to the endless ages."

> Jesus, such His love and power,
>   Such His presence dear,
> Everywhere and every hour
>   With His own is near;
>
> With the glorified at rest
>   Far in Paradise,
> With the pilgrim saints distress'd
>   'Neath these cloudier skies;
>
> With the ransom'd soul that flew
>   From the cross to heaven,
> With the Emmaus travellers two,
>   With the lake-borne seven.
>
> Lord, Thy promise Thou wilt keep,
>   Thine shall dwell with Thee,
> And, awaking or asleep,
>   Thus together be.

XI

THE MORNING MEAL—LOVEST THOU ME?

Jesus says to them, Come, break your fast. None of the disciples ventured to question Him, Who art Thou? knowing that it is the Lord. So Jesus comes, and takes the bread and gives it to them, and the fish in the same way. This was the now third manifestation of Jesus to His disciples, as risen from the dead.

The fishes were numbered, and Peter's work was done. And now the reticent Master speaks again; and with the word He approaches (ver. 14) the fire, evidently from a position beyond it, as the disciples looked from the beach landwards. As they sit near Him He personally dispenses the morning meal. Apparently it was a silent time. A spell was upon the Seven; a sense of awe even greater than on former occasions of interview in these blessed days. And no wonder; for at each successive time, surely, something said to them, as they looked and listened, that the Lord was nearer to His glory.

So He, none other than Himself, and by no intermediary, fed them. And He is the same still. From some points of view there is, and must be, much intermediate agency in the carrying about in the world the message and the ordinances of the Lord. Men must translate the Scriptures, and labour in their publication and exposition. Men must minister to other men the Sealing Rites of the blessed message. But in the ultimate truth of the matter nothing but Christ is the soul's aliment, and none but Christ, through the work of His Holy Spirit, is the Host, the Provider and Dispenser of Himself. "I will come in, and will sup with him, and he with Me" (Rev. iii. 20).

This then was *the third* appearance, *the third* time. The statement is meant, of course, to stand in relation to the whole of this Johannine narrative of the Resurrection period. It thus means obviously that this was the third appearance to any considerable gathering of the disciples, as on the Easter evening, and on that day week, when Thomas was brought to believe. Neither John nor the Synoptists record, for certain, any other appearance *to a company* beside these three occasions and—what surely followed later than this—the meeting on the Galilean mountain (Matt. xxviii.), and then the meeting before, and at, the Ascension. This "third time" needs notice only as an example of the way in which Scripture expects us, if I may say so, to use our common sense in its explanation. Pressed literally, these words of St John may seem to contradict other records. Taken with remembrance of the context, which the thoughtful reader is assumed to remember, the agreement with the whole record is complete.

Such, then, was that third interview. There sate that favoured group before the Master, on the level margin of the lake, in the stillness of the morning, after the night of toil; and "ate and drank with Him after He had risen from the dead" (Acts x. 41), and knew it was He. A silence, as we have said, seemed to lie upon them. It was a silence of awe, yet also of rest. "In that hour they asked Him nothing," because they saw, because they knew.

Toil was over, and so also was unconsciousness of His presence, and doubt about it. There is much in the whole fair scene to make us believe it to be, besides its inestimable value as a record of fact, also a picture, drawn by the Saviour's own hand, of the eternal festival beyond the waves of labour and strife, where "they hunger and thirst no more," and where yet "the Lamb shepherds them, and leads them to the living fountains" (Rev. vii. 16, 17). That blissful hour "is prepared as the morning." Silently as the rising of the day, but as surely too, it is coming, it will be here. Shall we not all be found there through grace, leaving the night and the deep behind us, and feeling the Sun of eternal joy rise on us, and on the Land of our desire, as we feast in and on the manifested presence of the beloved Lord?

But St John leaves the lesson, the mystery, to be drawn out by the reader, and passes on at once.

So when they had broken their fast, Jesus says to Simon Peter, Simon, son of Jonah am I dear to you more than to these? He says to Him, Yes, Lord, Thou *knowest that I love* Thee. *He says to Him, Feed My lambs. Again He says to Him, a second time, Simon, son of Jonah, am I dear to you? He says to Him, Yes, Lord.* Thou *knowest that I love* Thee. *He says to Him, Shepherd My dear sheep* (προβάτια). *He says to him the third time, Simon, son of Jonah, do you love Me? Peter was pained that He said to him the third time,*

Do you love Me? And he said to Him, Lord, Thou *knowest* (οἶδας) *all things;* Thou *seest* (γινώσκεις) *that I love Thee. Jesus says to him, Feed My dear sheep.*

The silent meal was over then, and Jesus speaks. He speaks so as indeed to answer fully the unspoken question, if they had felt it stir within them, *Who art Thou?* He who now speaks is indeed THE LORD.

Peter is addressed. He has been already conspicuous in the scene; plunging into the lake while the others row shoreward, climbing into the beached boat, and drawing in the net. Now he is singled out to be for a while the one figure, with Jesus, in our view. And this is done (the Lord often does so still in His grace and providence) so as to leave the disciple at once humble and happy.

We may suppose that Peter needed both humiliation and happiness specially just then. His haste to reach the shore may have had in it some slight trace of personal display of devotion. And on the other hand there was a deep wound in his soul, left by the denials of that remembered and recent night of terror In the complexities of that human heart there was possible room for both feelings at once; for a yielding once more to a self-asserting impulse, and for a sore sickness of soul in memory and conviction. Self-assertion and inmost sadness sometimes lie near together. And to both maladies the blessed Lord knows how to apply His searching, healing hand.

We are not to think that this was the first moment of Peter's restoration and acceptance. He was present on both the previous occasions when Jesus had met His disciples and had blessed them with His peace. He had enjoyed one secret interview, on the great Easter Day itself; *the Lord appeared unto Simon* (Luke xxiv. 34); an appearance which assuredly conveyed to the penitent Apostle, *in private*, a blessed restoration. But very deep griefs, especially of the conscience, may well ask for more than a solitary act and word of reassurance. In his pain and exhaustion the sufferer is thankful if the message may be "doubled unto him." And besides, in this case, the secret welcome back and the general benediction could not fully take the place of a public reinstatement of the lapsed Apostle, in view of his association with his brethren and, in some sense, leadership amongst them.

So the Lord deliberately and solemnly restored him, with His own lips, and before six Apostolic witnesses. The mighty wound needed a proportionate remedy. And the remedy was to be such as also to remind him for ever of his snares and his weakness, that he might watch and stand.

Verse 15. *Simon, (son) of Jonah, am I dear to you?*

"Simon, son of Jonah." It is almost exactly the same phrase as that used in St John's first chapter (ver. 42); only a little briefer, by the omission of "son," as was natural in a direct appellation. The appellation occurs nowhere else in this Gospel, often as Peter is referred to in its narratives. The use of the words here is assuredly by design, and observable; the Lord uses on purpose in this restitution of the Apostle the name which He had used at his first call. He reminds Peter thus that he must be content to start anew, to begin again as the catechumen; not Cephas now, not Peter now, for the time, but just Simon, Jonah's son.

And the question put by the Lord is as elementary as the appellation: ἀγαπᾷς με πλεῖον τούτων; *Do you love Me more than these others do?* It is possible, grammatically, I hardly need say, to explain the Greek either thus, or, *Do you love Me more than you love these men?* But surely of the two renderings the latter is not to the purpose of the occasion.

Nothing in the narrative suggests any special need that the Lord should, as it were, lay His hand on Peter and ask him if he could prefer Him to his Apostolic friends. But the other explanation fits exactly into the picture as we have it: "Is your love to Me warmer, stronger, higher than theirs?" The old weakness of Peter's heart was its tendency to profess a peculiar and superior love. "Though all should deny Thee, yet will not I; I will never be offended." So he had said just before his fall; self-assertion had gone before, close before, what had indeed seemed to be his utter ruin. He had not been willing to love, to trust, to follow, quite simply; he must needs do so with a mind full of estimates of comparison favourable to himself: "My love, my obedience, see what they are; admire the devoted Apostle!" It is a mysterious possibility, the lingering of such thoughts in the same soul which at the same time in a measure feels, and utters, true love to its Redeemer. But it is as true as it is mysterious. And what shall be the antidote? Nothing but such a God-given view of Him in His beauty and glory as shall draw the soul clear off from a centre in itself to rest, not in an abstract self-oblivion, but in Him. To shake off the consciousness of our personality is the dream of the pantheist. The self-denial of the Gospel comes when the individual so sees and receives Christ that HE occupies and fills the personality with the power and peace of His living presence. Then indeed it lives; lives individually, lives with rich developments of character, yet lives purely and simply, because in and by the Lord. The more it is thus with the man the less will he be betrayed into the hollow and unhappy thought, "I love Him better than others do; I serve more, I bear more in His name, than others."

Such surely, be it said with all reverence for the blessed Apostle's sacred memory, had been the special risk for St Peter. And upon this now the Master lays His firm and loving hand, in the question: *Am I dear to you, more than to these?*

I venture to render ἀγαπᾶς με thus: *Am I dear to you?* It may at least remind us that there *is* a difference here in the Greek words rendered "love" in our version: ἀγαπᾶν, φιλεῖν. But it can only express imperfectly the generally recognized distinction, that ἀγαπᾶν, on the whole, denotes the more deliberate affection and φιλεῖν the warmer emotion. Archbishop Trench gives careful attention to the distinction in his *New Testament Synonyms*, a book which is often the best of commentaries on a difficult text; and his conclusion is as I have just said. Thus here the Lord asks the Apostle, in His first two queries, whether he loves Him in the clear, exalted way of the soul's full choice and calm satisfaction, and the Apostle, surely as owning himself unworthy to assert so serene and sublime an affection, feeling himself inadequate to it, sinner that he is, replies in the other word, so warm, so personal, but also humble; φιλῶ σε, I love Thee with my poor heart's love. My paraphrase does but doubtfully express this, but it can point to it. Let me only add, as regards the study of the two words, that the distinction is by no means to be pressed generally. The two verbs, when either occurs apart, are apt each to absorb something of the other's meaning. It is when placed together, as here, that their distinction must be carefully remembered.

Simon, son of Jonah, am I dear to you? So says the Lord Jesus twice over to His servant. Am I dear to you? Does your heart, with a strong, full choice of love and gladness, choose Me? Does it rest in Me, as all its salvation and also as all its desire? Ἀγαπᾷς με? Wonderful question! We cannot but remark it, as we pass on, as an instance of the mysterious, persistent "self-assertion" of the Lord. He mentions not the word GOD. It occurs but once in this

chapter, and then not in His utterances. It is
"*I*," "*Me*," "till *I* come," "*My* sheep," "*My*
lambs*,*" "lovest thou *Me?*" Let us observe
this with reverent attention. It is one of the
deepest implicit proofs of the Divine Oneness of
the Father and the Son, this tone and claim of
the Son about Himself which, but for the truth
of the *Homoüsion*, the Co-essentiality, would be
nothing else than the intrusion of an alien
medium between the soul and the Maker, the
claim of a love for the creature, however exalted
a creature this might be, which is due only to
the Creator, who is blessed for ever.

"Am I dear to thee, in the dearness of this
lofty affection, this ἀγάπη?" Wonderful question, let us say it again; wonderful from this
other point of view, that it shows such a care
on HIS part for the love of such poor hearts as
ours. It is indeed lovable in JESUS CHRIST
that He loves us to love Him; that it is something to HIM that the sinful human being who
a few weeks earlier had denied acquaintance
with Him should return now, not with terror
and despair, but with love, to His blessed side.
"Give me thine *heart*" is the most searching,
as it is the most characteristic, of the demands
of the God of Revelation, of the God of Christ,
of Christ the Son of God. But it is also a

demand infinitely amiable. He who thus asks for the gift of the heart has on His part a heart to give. "Lovest thou Me? I care that thou shouldest love Me. Read in My question the truth, the certainty, that I loved thee, that I love thee."

Let me quote the words of one of the greatest of modern preachers, as he was one of the most devoted and loving of modern believers, Adolphe Monod; words in his Sermon entitled, *Dieu démandant le cœur à l'Homme:* "No other religion presents anything which resembles this invitation to give God the heart. Give me thy observances, says the God of Pharisaism. Give me thy personality, says the God of Hegel. Give me thy reason, says the God of Kant. ... It remains for the God of Jesus Christ to say, Give Me thy heart. ... He makes it the essence and the glory of His doctrine. With Him, to give the heart to God is not merely an obligation of piety; it is its root, its beginning, its middle, and its end. It is the unmistakable feature (*le caractère non équivoque*) of a genuine conversion. You tell me that a man believes the Gospel of grace; he does well, but does he believe it with a living faith? You tell me that he is in the front of every Christian effort; ay, but does he bring with him a Christian spirit?

But tell me that he has given his heart to God, and every other question is superfluous. Faith, works, grace, holiness, the new creation, all is there. Will you enter on the possession?"

"Am I dear to you?" Such was the question put by Jesus to Peter, on the shore, by the fire, in the presence of Peter's six listening friends. It was a strangely searching moment. The night was over, with all its movements, its excitements, its lassitude; Peter's stirring, leading spirit is for a while in check; and now, before his Master and his friends, he is faced by this question altogether of the heart, the inner heart, not of the outer act: "Am I dear to you?" Let us sit reverently down beside the Apostle, and humbly put ourselves also in the line of that question. Let us often listen for it; and not least after some hour of vivid interest, of strong exertion, of rich intercourse. Then, if ever, let us sit down before the Lord and hear Him say, "Am I dear to you?" Do not ask others whether they think you love Christ. Let Christ ask you. Friends will be very kind and indulgent in their answers for us; at least, so it will be if they are themselves humble believers. They will give us more than full credit for every work we try to do under the banner of religion, for every sacrifice we seem to make in a Christian cause. Yes, they will be kind; and so will the Lord Jesus be. Only, He will be omniscient also, and will not for a moment mistake act for motive, hand for heart. When He puts the question, we shall have to reply with Peter, *Lord, Thou knowest all things, Thou knowest*— what shall it be?—*that I love Thee?* Why should it not be so? If you love, not worthily (that is impossible) but really, you may surely *know* it. And why not love really? Nothing can prevent it but blindness to what Jesus Christ is, oblivion of what Jesus Christ is and does for you.

Oh, sweet it is to know, most simply, that the soul loves Him; not as it should love Him, truly, and not "more than these," with a glance of self-consciousness around; but that indeed it does love Him—whether ἀγαπῶ or φιλῶ be its chosen word.

St Peter happily could answer at once, before his Lord and his companions, *Yes, Lord, Thou knowest that I love Thee.* Φιλῶ σε. The stress is on "I love," not on "Thee." And the φιλῶ is emphatic, as I have said above; it indicates a certain avoidance of the other verb. "I love Thee, with such love as this poor heart can feel. I speak not of the heights of heavenly affection now. But Thou knowest, my Lord, my Saviour, that *I do love Thee*, with most personal devotion."

No utterance could have been more beautifully in keeping with that hour of mysterious agitation and solemn joy. It was otherwise with Peter in later days. In his First Epistle, that golden document of the Gospel, he says without reserve, of all true believers, *Him having not seen ye love* (ἀγαπᾶτε). But here, by the lake, what could have been more true to all the wonderful surroundings than this φιλῶ σε? And we observe that the Lord, in His third enquiry, concedes this word to the Apostle. He meets him, He condescends to him, half-way. "*Simon, son of Jonah, do you love Me?* Φιλεῖς με? I note your chosen word; I understand your choice; and now I am content to put My question in your way. I ask you now for one final assurance thus—φιλεῖς με?"

Let us too hear our blessed Master put to us His question in those terms. If indeed φιλεῖν is in so far lower than ἀγαπᾶν that it indicates less of insight and more of emotion, yet the word, though lower by comparison, is in itself a precious word. "Do you feel a loving affection for Me?" Do we? Are we not somewhat too easily content to dispense with that experience? In a just anxiety not to build our salvation on our feelings (and indeed we need to be very clear upon that matter) let us not forget the other side. Let us not forget that exactly because our peace is built not on our feelings but on our most adorable and loving Lord, therefore it is for us to draw from it, in the glad necessity of a true spiritual sequence, the result of an ardent affection in the inmost heart.

> I love Thee for the glorious worth
> In Thy great Self I see;
> I love Thee for the shameful Cross
> Thou hast endured for me.

If we believe, if we enter into the truths, let me say, of the Nicene Creed, that blessed summary of truth and love, worthy of often repetition in private, as well as before the Table of the Lord, shall not the words of our confession of His Name be inbreathed all through with the secret consciousness, strong and reverently tender, ἀγαπῶ σε, Κύριε, φιλῶ σε, Κύριε?

I have not attempted to take up *seriatim* the three questions and three answers. The *thrice-*repeated enquiry seems to carry so manifest a reference to the threefold denial, and a reference of that suppressed and implicit kind characteristic of St John's record, that it is surprising that a doubt should ever have been cast on the reference. What to my own mind makes it certain is the whole character of the scene. It is a solemn reinstatement of St Peter, not merely into right relations with his Master generally, but into Apostolic relations with Him. Certainly it was *not* a commission to him to be the Prince of the Apostles, the universal Bishop.[1] Were it so, Peter was most unfaithful to his commission; for never, by written word or recorded deed, did he claim even the shadow of such a power. But the Saint, though he receives no commission here to be lord over his brethren, does receive a threefold assurance of his full restoration to a sacred place among his brethren. "Be a feeder of My lambs, the weak, the young; be a tending watchman of My dear flock. In all the fulness of the privilege, the labour, and the peril, be again My own Apostle, till at the last you are My Martyr."

I must not at present follow out further the details of this part of the passage. I close now with one obvious remark of application to ourselves. The Lord's questions to Peter about

---

[1] It is curious to read here in M. Lasserre's often excellent modern French rendering of the Gospels the significant words, *Sois* le *pasteur de mes agneaux, Sois* le *pasteur de mes brebis.* The version of the Jansenist de Saci reads simply *Paissez mes agneaux, Paissez mes brebis.*

love to Himself are each at once followed by a command, a command to help the souls of others. From this, two reflections naturally arise, and with them we will once more withdraw for a season from that holy group on the Galilean beach.

First, the great qualification for work for Christ in the hearts of others is love to Christ in the worker's heart, real, personal love in the conscious individual experience.

Then, secondly, where that love is present, kindled by His free and wonderful love to us, there we may expect as the sure sequel that some work for Him in the hearts of others will be put by Him into our hands. He lights the holy flame. He also lays on the fuel which will draw out its life and power.

Happy the Christian who, in the path not of self-choice but of the guidance of God, finds evermore both truths exemplified; love of the Saviour animating work for Him, work for Him giving movement, and expansion, and permanence, to the sense of love.

XII

THE MASTER AND HIS SERVANTS.

IN the previous chapter we studied the narrative of St Peter's three confessions of love to his Master, and his Master's thrice-repeated restoration and commission of him as a shepherd of the flock. Without returning at any length to that scene, I notice two or three detached points in it.

(i.) The use of the words φιλεῖν and ἀγαπᾶν. Is this an incidental evidence that our Lord sometimes used the Greek language in conversation with His own friends? The Aramaic has no parallel distinction of verbs; and, on the other hand, no one who reads St John's style with attention can well doubt that a distinction of verbs is intended here by him. The late Dr A. Roberts, one of the New Testament Revisers, in his *Discussions on the Gospels*, has made out a very interesting case for the familiar use of Greek in Palestine about the time of the First Advent; and he thinks that we have here a narrative which implies such use. Undoubtedly Aramaic was in large and frequent use. Again and again the Saviour's Aramaic words to individuals are recorded; and St Paul delivered a long address in Aramaic to the crowds in the Temple court. But are not these incidents so recorded as to suggest that the rule was, at least, very often broken? In any case, Greek *was* spoken, very much as English is spoken in Ireland. And why should not the Lord Jesus have employed it on this occasion, even if His usage were the other way, if only to bring out a sacred lesson as to different qualities of love? On the other hand, even should it be shewn beyond doubt that Aramaic was spoken that morning by the lake, we need not regard the difference of verbs in the Greek record as unimportant. I should then venture to think that the Holy Inspirer, guiding the Apostle's mind, led him to the use of words which would bring out the thought, the *animus*, of the colloquy more clearly than a verbatim record would have done, leaving out as *it* must the explanations given by the voices and manner of the speakers. But I do not think we need doubt that Greek was that language of the hour.

(ii.) As to the actual avowal by St Peter of φιλία not ἀγάπη. Bishop Wordsworth takes the view suggested in the last chapter—that self-distrust and a sacred sense of the Lord's glory leads St Peter to his φιλῶ σε, and bids him shrink from ἀγαπῶ σε, as an utterance too lofty for his deeply humbled heart. The Bishop remarks very beautifully (a little was said in the last chapter in this direction) that the Saviour, while accepting at last Peter's lower word, yet knew that he would have grace to live the higher word. Wonderfully is this illustrated by the Saint's precious Epistles. Where does the New Testament breathe a more serene and heavenly love for the Lord than there? And yet it is a love intense and individual too—φιλία at the heart of ἀγάπη: "Him ye *love* (ἀγαπᾶτε) with *joy* unspeakable" (1 Pet. i. 8). So let it be with each Christian generation and each Christian heart. The steadfast, heaven-given choice of Christ and rest in Him must have within it also the sacred emotion of personal and grateful delight. Ever to the end, and beyond the end, shall we be saying, as we look on HIM, φιλῶ σε, Κύριε.

(iii.) The Commission to Peter: "Feed My lambs—My sheep; shepherd My sheep." Perhaps the word "lambs" is not, so to speak, separative here, marking off a class different from the "sheep." It may be just the προβάτια from another point of view; much as in 1 John ii., where surely "Fathers," "Youths," "Little ones," are terms descriptive of true disciples from different *sides*. All the Lord's sheep are in some respects "lambs"; tender and adolescent to the end, compared with what they shall be hereafter. Yet it is impossible not to read in the words at least a suggestion to the pastor to remember specially the specially lamb-like of the flock, the very weak and the very young.

(iv.) Let us remember too the twice-repeated "feed," βόσκε, which is thus indicated as the main particular in the "shepherding." Feed them, give them provender; that food which is the Lord Himself, beheld, believed, received, beloved. Let this be the Alpha and Omega of the Christian minister's shepherding, whatever else goes with it as assistant and subsidiary. "The hungry sheep look up and *are not fed*," says Milton in a well-known passage, stigmatizing the unfaithful, unspiritual pastors of his young days. Do not let the words be true of the Lord's shepherds now. It is all too possible to keep the flock of Christ in a most undesirable sort of *fast*, both in and out of Lent; a fast from Christ set forth before them in His finished sacrifice, and never-ending life, love, and power.

Would the clergy be safe from the risk of

proving, whether they know it or not, starvation preachers? Then let them every day, "with keen despatch of real hunger," be found feeding for themselves on Christ Jesus the Lord. *Unde vivo, inde dico; in quo pascor, hoc ministro.*

(v.) Lastly, observe the Lord's phrase, τά ἀρνία μου, MY lambs, MY flock, not thine. It is too easy in practice to forget it. There is a sense in which of course the man must think of class, school, parish, church, as "mine"; in the sense of personal responsibility and heart interest. But much more still must he watch and pray that he may think of them all as "Thine." And to do so will be a powerful and manifold assistance in the ministry. It will cheer, solemnize, tranquillize the pastor. It will cheer him, as reminding him that his Lord's interest in his charge is far deeper than his own can be. It will solemnize him, as reminding him of his own intensely direct relations with his Lord as His underling. It will tranquillize him, because there is nothing which more distracts us and disturbs us than self-consciousness and self-love, nothing which more settles and strengthens us than simple love to Him. Realizing that the flock, the sheep, the lambs, are HIS, we pastors shall labour for them more purely and more happily; and we shall also be more ready if it should please Him to put us and our efforts quite aside, and to hand the dear charge over to another. They are His; we are His. For the under-shepherd is himself also (blessed thought) one of the Chief Shepherd's flock.

But now without delay let us pass onward to the pregnant conclusion of the narrative.

Verse 18. The Saviour couples at once with His commission to Peter the prediction for him of a martyr's death. It comes with all the solemnity of the double *Verily*. *Verily, verily, I say to you, when you were a younger man, you were used to tie your own girdle, and to walk where you would; but when you have grown old, you shall stretch out your hands, and another shall tie your girdle, and carry you where you would not. Now this He said, as indicating by what sort of death he was to glorify God. And with that word He says to him, Follow Me.*

A remark or two on words and construction is called for. *When you were a younger man.* The Lord Jesus is referring to the time of Peter's life then present. Just such an act of free choice and vigorous independent motion had Peter that morning done, when he had "*girt* his upper coat upon him, and *thrown himself* into the lake." "*When you were*" is an anticipatory phrase, a prolepsis; it looks back as if already from the time of Peter's death. (Parallels are not unfrequent; see the interesting one, 1 Cor. xiii. 12 : "Then shall I know even as I *was* known," καθὼς καὶ ἐπεγνώσθην). "In the days of thy youth" is the practical meaning of the expression. There seems to be at least a high likelihood, as we have repeatedly noticed, that the Apostles were very much of an age with their blessed Master. Conventional art has usually represented them as all, excepting St John, men of elderly years. Far more probably they were at most thirty-five years old; a probability which may help us to understand them on many occasions in their impulses and mistakes.

In the days of thy youth, then; the days now fast passing, to be followed so soon by the far different and quickly aging life of the Apostolic evangelist and pastor. He had been used to choose his own path in those days, in these days. But a change should come; he should live to be old; and then, on some special occasion, in some memorable way, he should choose the path no more. He should stretch out his hands, and another should gird him; and the path should be one which he did not choose, a path against his choice, and along which he should be *carried*.

We now well know what the Lord meant, whatever at the moment these first hearers understood in detail. St John at once applies them to his friend's death, and to that death as a special occasion of the glorification of God, and as evidently caused by man—that is, a martyr death. The future, δοξάσει, "shall glorify," does not imply (I hardly need say) that the event was still future when John wrote; it was only future when Jesus spoke. It is practically quite certain that many years before this narrative was written at Ephesus Peter had died unto the Lord: the prophecy had been fully expounded by the event. And we need not doubt that the death was by crucifixion; indeed, the words here about the outstretched hands may assure us of this. The well-known further particulars of the martyrdom, that it was at Rome (where now stands the Church of S. Pietro in Montorio, on the far-seeing Janiculan), and that the Saint died head downwards, rest on a very different quality of evidence; though we need not seriously doubt about Rome as the locality. As to the inverted attitude, it is Origen who first, of extant writers, speaks of it: and he wrote five generations later. It may have been.

Where you do not choose—to a death of violence and pain. Yes, let us remember this.

Peter, the saint indeed, did not choose pain as pain and death as death. That is the act of mental and spiritual aberration. What he did choose was obedience to his Lord, fidelity to his Lord, and then the Lord's glorious presence after that painful passage to it. But from *the passage* human nature shrank in Peter, even as the Lord Himself in His own true Human Nature, absolutely identical with ours, had shrunk from His own agony. I allude to this manifest fact in passing, because it is an instance of what we everywhere find in Scripture, the deeply and truly *natural* aspect in which, in it, the Christian life is presented. That life is not the extinction of nature; it is its transfiguration, as the heart's love and the will's choice are fixed upon the supreme and all-satisfying Object. It does not make man unhuman. It is a new man, but still man. And man, as man, never can like pain, or grief, or death, for its own sake.

This obvious remark has a bearing on the value of the earliest Christian martyrdoms as a testimony to the Gospel truth. Had they been theatrical displays of unnatural courage they would have borne feeble witness to the solidity of the facts which the martyrs confessed, and for confessing which they died. The body might in that case have been given to the stoning, or the steel, by a motive no better than a diseased spiritual ambition, a personal and emulous desire for a high place in the coming glory as the reward of special pain. But Stephen, James, Peter, and Paul died not so. They did not choose or court death. They chose Christ and His truth, and died rather than deny it. And here, in their calmness and spiritual sanity, in their willingness not to die if it could be avoided rightly, lies the weight and power of their *witness*, their μαρτυρία. It appears as a witness indeed; not a display of their courage so much as an indication of the strong solidity of the basis of truth beneath their feet.

We cannot but recall that one other legend of St Peter's last scenes, the *Domine, quo vadis?* Many of my readers may have pondered it with emotion near its alleged place of occurrence, just outside Rome, on the Appian Way. St Ambrose gives it to us—at the distance of three centuries from St Peter; but however uncertain in fact, it illustrates precious truths with pathetic power. The Apostle was condemned. The Roman Christians entreated and persuaded him to accept an opportunity of escape; an escape which was certainly no crime in itself. But the Lord's call to death and glory had now come at last; and at the gate of the City, in the grey morning, as the old man passed out, he met a Stranger passing in; and behold it was the Lord. "Lord, whither goest Thou?"—"I go to be crucified in thy place." Peter returned to his prison, and to the cross, and by his death glorified God.

They shall carry you where you would not. It is remarkable indeed, this solemn prophecy of suffering, so closely connected with the joy of love and restoration. In one way or another it will surely be thus with every true disciple of our beloved Saviour. To each of us without exception He will assign some cross to bear for Him; to each He will say, in one way or another, "If you love Me, serve Me; and you shall *suffer for Me.*" Only, the suffering is the "accident," the joy the "substance." First the pardon, the love, the gladness; then the allotment of the cross, which that deep joy will make so much better than bearable. Peter was not to be martyred that he might win the love of Christ, but because he had obtained it. The order is, indeed, "first cross, then crown." But the cross is preceded by the embrace of the eternal arms. *Crucem porta, te portabit,* is a beautiful motto; but let us not confuse its meaning. The cross we carry is our cross of trial, the cross where self is crucified. The cross which carries us is the Lord's Cross of atonement, the Cross of complete salvation. If in any sense our cross can be truly said to carry us, it can only be as it is a means to teach us how to realize better our repose on His.

So Peter received this solemn outline of his future. Strange privilege, to be permitted to know in advance just so much of "the unknown to-morrow"! Probably the whole meaning of the prediction was not at once clear to him, or to John. But at once, surely, they recognized in it a prediction, distinct and supernatural, of long service closed by violent death. Such an expectation then Peter carried with him all his life, and close to the end he refers definitely to it (2 Pet. i. 14): "*Sudden is to be the putting off of my tabernacle, even as our Lord Jesus Christ once shewed me.*" Yet we may be sure that this knowledge of his predestined course and goal gave no unreality to his life, to his methods of work, to his precautions for safety, to his thoughts of death. Like many other divine purposes, it was indicated just so far as to reveal the infallible purpose, and yet to leave the man as consciously free as ever step by step. God knows how to make His counsel work freely in absolute harmony with the creature's genuine agency.

The Lord had said, *Follow Me* (ἀκολούθει μοι), an exhortation which but for the context we might have thought to be general (for observe the *present* imperative) and figurative. And so no doubt it was in great part. "If any man serve Me, let him follow Me"—let him live near Me, watch My will and learn My way. But the utterance was, however, illustrated by an act. We gather that the Lord Jesus *moved*, walking away along the shore or towards the hill, and bade Peter literally follow Him. The command was not, so far as it appears, meant for the whole party. Only Peter is addressed, and Peter is surprised to see John following also. The whole incident must have been brief and symbolic. Let us translate the verses.

Peter turning round (as he stepped forward after his Master, evidently, and heard steps behind him), *sees the disciple whom Jesus loved following, the disciple who also had leaned over at the supper to Him and said, Lord, who is Thy betrayer? Seeing him Peter says to Jesus, Lord, but what of him? Jesus says to him, If I choose that he remain till I come, how does it affect you? Do you follow*

Me. So this report went out to the brethren, that that disciple is not to die. And yet Jesus did not say to him that he was not to die, but, If I choose that he remain till I come, how does it affect you?

This is the disciple who witnesses about these things, and who wrote these things; and we know that his witness is true.

Now there are many other things too which Jesus did, things which if they were written each in detail not even the world itself, I think, would have room for the books which would be writing.

One word, out of place, on the last two verses. Without any attempt at explicit critical discussion, I would only say that they seem to me to be written by St John himself, not added later by other hands. "*We know*" is a turn of expression quite in the Apostle's manner; he loves to put himself as it were aside; to speak as *ab extra* of himself. And surely, had the Ephesian Church thought it needful, or decorous, to add an *imprimatur* to an Apostle's writing, they would not have expressed themselves so simply. *The disciple* would scarcely have been in their view an adequate description for their blessed patriarch and guide, the personal friend of their Divine

Redeemer. Moreover, they would hardly have added an attestation while John lived ; and had they done so after his death, could they have left the mysterious words which had prompted the rumour of his immortality without some further comment?

As regards the hyperbole in which is conveyed the thought that to record all the Lord Jesus did would be " infinite "—the phrase *is* an hyperbole, no doubt. But if plainly intended to be so taken, it is perfectly veracious. It most manifestly is not a prosaic estimate of the area which the books would cover.

Far better than any lingering over such a verbal difficulty is an application to the heart of what the phrase imports. It tells us that such was the boundless wealth of the Lord's works of love and power that even the precious Gospel of St John is but a brief selection, divinely ordered yet quite brief, from out of the wealth. Let us give thanks both for the wealth of the materials, and for the brevity of the record—a brevity so good for the busy and for the simple reader. Abundantly enough is written to serve the holy purpose of the writer —*that we may believe that Jesus is the Christ, the Son of God, and that, believing, we may have life in His name.*

But now to return to the narrative of verses 20—22.

We have seen, early in our study, how the hearts of Peter and John had been drawn together. Together we find the two Saints in their Passover-lodging, together at the tomb, together on the waters, together soon at the Beautiful Gate, together before the Council, together at Samaria. The last Gospel closes with this scene in which they follow their Lord together, yet in which their Lord reminds them how different at length their ways of following should be.

Peter, it would seem, had risen to follow, and then John, as he sat close to his earthly friend and to that heavenly Friend who bound them together, silently rose and followed too, while perhaps the other disciples as yet did not move. As always, John is not named; he is described as the loved disciple, and as the man who, as he reclined at the supper, leaned nearer to the Lord, and asked Him about the traitor. Why this last detail is introduced here it is not easy to say. Peter on that occasion had been the enquirer through John. So it *may* be that the event is here mentioned as an occasion on which they had acted together. Or is it simply that the incident was an example of the near intimacy between John and his beloved Master?

So Peter turns, and sees John following. And now, full of the thought of the prediction of his own martyrdom, and instinctively connecting all that concerned himself with the concerns of his dear and ever dearer companion, he asks what *his* end shall be. Οὗτος δὲ τί; What should *he* do? Shall he also grow old, and then stretch out his hands, and be carried where he fain would not go? He is following Thee, and me, now with his steps. Shall he follow also in the manner of his life, and of his death?

I need not dwell at length on the Lord's memorable answer. At first sight at least it reads very simply, as if just a grave and gentle correction of Peter's too anxious curiosity, or at most a gentle reminder that his truest peace would be found in following personally his Redeemer in the path chosen for *him*, leaving John's path to the same choice. There may undoubtedly be a deeper meaning. It may be that the "coming" of the Son of man when the City, and Temple, and Ritual passed away—His mystical Advent in judgment and mercy then—was intended. It is at least very probable that St John was the only Apostle who survived the year 70, and that he survived it long, living far on into the new age of the Christian Church.

We must observe, however, that the first disciples plainly took the "Till I come" to refer to the great literal Second Coming, the Era of immortality; for they reasoned from the words that John would not die. He was to abide till the Lord came; therefore till the Resurrection; therefore he would not sleep, but be changed. And the old Apostle, so it seems to me, corrects the error by calling attention to the emphatic "*if*" (ἐάν) of the sentence as the Lord spoke it, and to the "What is that to thee?"

Likely as we must feel it to be that these solemn final words of the last Gospel should have a deeper meaning than the literal, I cannot think that we can be certain that it is so. The great age reached by St John before this record was written had very possibly given them an emphasis and mystery among "the brethren" which was beyond their first intention.

I love to think, though it may be too arbitrary a thought, that the Apostle here takes pains to correct any misconception, because, in part, of his own deep longing to be with the Lord. He would not linger on in an earthly immortality. He would thankfully pass through the gate of death, as Peter long ago had done, as yet longer ago his Lord Himself had done, to be soon and for ever with Him where He is.

If I will. Let us close by an act of solemn attention to these words. Some time ago we observed how markedly, all through this chapter, Jesus speaks of and from Himself: *Lovest thou Me? Feed My flock: Follow Me: Till I come: If I will.*

Who is this who, if He speaks not blasphemy, speaks in His own right with the voice of GOD?

If I will. "My will is to rule your future, Peter, and John's future too." Those precious lives, those regenerated and inspired apostolic souls, were to accept the predestination of their time and their labour from the mere will of Jesus. There is no fear lest that will and His Father's should differ, should collide; yet none the less is His will *His will.* And that will disposes absolutely of Peter and of John. They love, adore, and follow. It ordains.

He wills that the one, the eager, the impetuous, but now wonderfully chastened, the man of strong act and word, should spend for Him many years of heavy labour and much suffering, and then die for Him, in a death of extreme agony.

He wills that the other, the man of deep and silent spiritual life and thought, the character which we might perhaps have deemed to be "not long for this world," as the phrase is, should live on and on, working, suffering, thinking, writing, till every one of his comrades had fallen asleep, and should then die the death of all men.

The destiny of St John may remind us how deeply hidden are the details of the Lord's plans for His servants; how impossible it is for us to forecast their future by temperament or circumstance. We know a friend born and made as if for vigorous and sustained action. We know another of almost unearthly walk with God. But we know not which will be taken, and which left; or whether both will go early, or both very late. We have no hint whatever of the principles on which in these matters the Master acts. Certainly He is not capricious; but certainly also He has no such *need* of our character or labours as to allow the most laborious or the most successful Christian to say, "He cannot spare me yet."

But the great thing is to know, as we do know, that all shall be as "I WILL." There is a Will, there is a Person, above and beneath all our lives and works; and that Will, that Person, is Jesus our Lord. He and not fate, He and not chance, He and not the processes of an impersonal universe, at this hour rules and ordains our path of service, present and future; yes, and the path too of those we love, and about whom we sometimes ask more wistfully than about ourselves, *Lord, and what shall this man do?* Let us calmly and most thankfully recollect it. Bewildered souls try too often to find rest in absolute abject deference to the will of a poor fallen, erring man. It is the distortion into woful error of a glorious and most healthful truth. It *is* true rest to yield ourselves and our dear ones in entire simplicity, without a struggle or reserve, to the living will of the Lord Jesus Christ; for that will is omniscient, and all-wise, and all-holy, and (let us dare to believe it now and every hour) it is a will of such love that it does not for a minute forget, in the light of the glory of God, the true interests and true joy of the feeblest and most halting of the disciples.

Then let us, not so much think about Him as go direct to Him, to learn the secret which made Peter and John quite happy in their several paths; happy to work together, happy to work asunder. Their secret was, "It is the Lord; Thou hast loved me; Thou knowest that I love Thee."

So the one lived on till he had written, "Be sober, and hope to the end, for the grace that is to be brought unto you at the revelation of Jesus Christ."

So the other lived on, utterly alone at length in a new generation, a new world, but happy and sanctified to the end in the eternal truth, and able to write this about it: "Now are we the sons of God; and it doth not yet appear what we shall be, but we know that, when He shall appear, we shall be like Him, for we shall see Him as He is."

THE END.

APPENDICES.

I.

THE MESSAGE OF THE MAGDALENE
(p. 75).

" So from that happy grove,
From the still precincts of the Sepulchre,
She pass'd, obedient. Through the city streets
'Mid the first footfalls of the morn she went
Seeking the scatter'd brethren, and to each
With glad reiteration still in turn
Delivering the same story ;—she had seen
The Lord, and He had spoken thus to her.
 " Blest herald of redemption ! first to bear
Into these dying scenes of guilt and care
The tidings of that Sepulchre unseal'd ;
The marvel, the simplicity divine,
The nameless joy not dream'd of but reveal'd,
The eternal light we had not taught to shine,
Kindled by JESUS. She with one calm word
That she had seen arisen her buried Lord,
And from His lips had heard in that glad hour,
For those who left Him in His pain alone,
News not of wrath but of His rising power

And session for them on His Father's throne;
She first awoke the never-ending voice,
Redeemer, of Thy Gospel; the new song
In which innumerable souls rejoice,
Who, though in seeming triumph oft and long
Death wounds them, spoiling from their love's
    embrace
Its fondest treasures, and themselves meanwhile,
Claiming his prey, yet in Thy living grace
Find more than resignation—with a smile
Of strange delight discovering for their own
Thy sacrifice and resurrection-crown.

"She first, all happy Magdalena, bore
From Joseph's Grot the bliss unheard before,
And still her tidings was the broken tomb;
    And still, though ages roll,
    That message from the soul,
And that alone, must chase the enfolding gloom:
    Here still the worn and wandering mind
      Her true repose must find;
    Here learn the secret that can save;
      Beside, within, that Grave.

"Here still the heart can feel, and only here,
A tide of joy that brings no mingled fear
Of ebbing languor soon to fleet amain;—
    The soon exhausted life
    In faint and flagging strife
Seeking its vanish'd gladness to regain;—
    Not here from Fancy's haunted well
      Uncertain waters swell,
    But pour descending, never dry,
      From Truth's own fount on high.

" Yes, Truth indeed is here ; the Event divine,
O Saviour Lord, the Work that all is Thine ;
Once, once for all, with all its sequel, done ;
  Not in ourselves but Thee
  The almighty Cause we see
Which endless through its vast effects must run :
  Here we may trust to Thee the scope
   Of our undying hope ;
  Here we may know our doubts are vain ;
   For Thou art risen again.

" We by no far-drawn reasonings, brilliant
  length
But fragile, hold our Heaven. For us the strength
Of demonstration is the Risen One still;
  Our wisdom, science, all,
  Is at Thy feet to fall ;
Thou art our thought profound, our logic skill ;
  Our evidence of deathless bliss,
   Our earnest, still is this,
  That Thou hast shewn, from death restored,
   Thy face, beloved Lord.

" So let us tune, beneath the upkindling sphere,
Where stars on stars, Thy handiwork, appear,
Now gathering thick, our parting sound of praise ;
  Here midst the twinkling gloom,
  Here by this long-loved tomb,
Through Thee we antedate the eternal lays :
  'Tis here, above this precious dust,
   We sing Thee, as is just ;
  For by Thy Sepulchre this hour
   We overcome death's power.

" Thy Resurrection stands, and thence is cast
The smile of heaven o'er future, present, past ;

The Past is with Thy death-wrought victory
　　bright;
　　　　And though awhile we weep
　　　　The silence and the sleep,
Year after year, of those beyond our sight,
　　　　Yet not by drear misgivings torn
　　　　　Those buried loves we mourn;
　　　Seasons and times we count in vain,
　　　　But Thou art risen again.

"Then from that Truth an endless Future
　　springs,
　　Spiritual, real, throng'd with glorious things,
Peace, Resurrection, Heaven, for all Thine own;
　　　　With death we cheerly deal;
　　　　In thankful joy we kneel
Where shall be dress'd so soon our turf and stone:
　JESUS our Lord, the First and Last,
　　　　Thy rising work is past;
　　Then present is our strength and rest,
　　　And all our future, blest."
　　　　　　　　　　H. C. G. M.,
　　God's Acre (*Christianus and other Poems*).

II.

"EARTH LIGHTED UP FROM HEAVEN"

(p. 146).

　　　　"Though what if Earth
Be but the shadow of Heaven?"
　　　　　MILTON, *Paradise Lost*, v. 574.

" Acquaint thyself with God, if thou wouldst taste
　His works. Admitted once to His embrace
　Thou shalt perceive that thou wast blind before:...

[Well for] the mind that has been touch'd from
    Heaven,
And in the school of sacred wisdom taught
To read His wonders in whose thought the world,
Fair as it is, existed ere it was."
                COWPER, *The Task*, Book V.

" With Him for guide
Tracing the Paschal road (as oft we traced)
Along rich Ephraim's pastoral hills, I felt
Old Paradise restored ; in every field,
And mount, and lonely tree, a light of joy
Mingled of earth and heaven. The gleaming shores
Of my Gennesareth . . . shone with a charm
Unutterable, as if the curse indeed
Were cancell'd, and an earth beloved on high
Were made by only saints."
       H. C. G. M., *The Beloved Disciple, a Poem.*

" Heaven above is softer blue,
    Earth around is sweeter green ;
  Something lives in every hue
    Christless eyes have never seen ;
  Birds with gladder songs o'erflow,
    Flowers with deeper beauty shine,
  Since I know, as now I know,
    I am His and He is mine."
         WADE ROBINSON,
    Hymns of Consecration, No. 260.

"The Christians, as men who know God, ask from Him petitions which are proper for Him to give and for them to receive... And because they acknowledge the goodnesses of God towards them, lo, on account of them there flows forth the beauty that is in the world."

ARISTIDES, *Apology for the Christians, addressed to the Emperor Hadrian*, ch. xvi.

III.

MR RUSKIN ON THE INCIDENT OF JOHN XXI.

To introduce a severe critique of the splendid *conventionalism* of Raphael's "cartoon" of the scene, Mr Ruskin thus paints it:

"I SUPPOSE there is no event in the whole life of Christ to which, in hours of doubt or fear, men turn with more anxious thirst to know the close facts of it, or with more earnest and passionate dwelling upon every syllable of its recorded narrative, than Christ's showing Himself to His disciples at the Lake of Galilee. There is something pre-eminently open, natural, full fronting our disbelief, in this manifestation. The others, recorded after the Resurrection, were sudden, phantom-like, occurring to men in profound sorrow and wearied agitation of heart; not, it might seem, safe judges of what they saw.[1] But the agitation was now over. They had gone back to their daily work, thinking still their business lay net-wards, unmeshed from the literal rope and drag. 'Simon Peter saith unto them, I go a-fishing. They say unto him, We also go with thee.' True words enough, and having far echo beyond those Galilean hills. That night they caught nothing; but when the morn-

[1] This sentence must be taken with great reserve. It does not cover all the facts of Luke xxiv. and John xx.—H. C. G. M.

ing came, in the clear light of it, behold! a figure stood on the shore. They were not thinking of anything but their fruitless hauls. They had no guess who it was. It asked them simply if they had caught anything. They say, No; and it tells them to cast again. And John shades his eyes from the morning sun with his hands to look who it is; and though the glistening of the sea, too, dazzles him, he makes out who it is at last; and poor Simon, not to be outrun this time, tightens his fisher's-coat about him, and dashes in over the nets. One would have liked to see him swim those hundred yards, and stagger to his knees upon the beach.

"Well, the others get to the beach, too, in time, in such slow way as men in general do get in this world to its true shore, much impeded by that wonderful 'dragging the net with fishes'; but they get there—seven of them in all; first the Denier, and then the slowest believer, and then the quickest believer, and then the two throne-seekers, and two more, we know not who.

"They sit down on the shore, face to face with Him, and eat their broiled fish as He bids. And then to Peter, all dripping still, shivering, and amazed, staring at Christ in the sun, on the other side of the coal-fire,—thinking a little perhaps of what happened by another coal-fire, when it was colder, and having had no word changed with him by his Master since that look of His—to him so amazed, comes the question, 'Simon, lovest thou Me?' Try to feel that a little; and think of it till it is true to you."

Modern Painters; Part iv., ch. iv., § 16.
(Extracted also in *Frondes Agrestes*, p. 152.

www.ingramcontent.com/pod-product-compliance
Lightning Source LLC
Chambersburg PA
CBHW071439150426
43191CB00008B/1184